You're Welcome

Differentiating

Instruction

in the

Inclusive

Classroom

Patrick Schwarz
& Paula Kluth

HEINEMANN
Portsmouth, NH

To our fathers, Jimmy and Joseph,
For giving us the belief that doing good things
for people matters most.

Heinemann
A division of Reed Elsevier Inc.
361 Hanover Street
Portsmouth, NH 03801–3912
www.heinemann.com

Offices and agents throughout the world

Library of Congress Cataloging-in-Publication Data
Schwarz, Patrick.
    You're welcome : 30 innovative ideas for the inclusive classroom / Patrick Schwarz and Paula Kluth.
        p. cm.
    Includes bibliographical references.
    ISBN-13: 978-0-325-01204-9
    ISBN-10: 0-325-01204-0
    1. Individualized instruction—United States. 2. Inclusive education—United States.
3. Group work in education—United States. 4. Multicultural education—United States. I. Kluth, Paula. II. Title.

LB1031.S39 2007
371.9'046—dc22   2007016386

Editor: Harvey Daniels
Production: Lynne Costa
Cover design: Joni Doherty Design
Cover illustration: © Kevin Tolman/Photodisc/GettyImages
Typesetter: Kim Arney
Manufacturing: Louise Richardson

Printed in the United States of America on acid-free paper
11   10   09   08   07   CG   1   2   3   4   5

Contents

Acknowledgments

We are grateful to the many people who supported us to complete this project. Above all, we are indebted to the students with *possibilities* who have challenged us, taught us, and welcomed us into their lives over the years. We have been educated by many wonderful young people including Paul, Jason, Franklin, Tim, Mark, Jamie, Libby, Susan, Joe, Bob, Adam, Matt, John, Aaron, Andrew, and Bob.

The work of colleagues has also inspired this project, especially that of our dear colleague and friend, Alice Udvari-Solner. She has been a teacher to us for many years and constantly pushes our thinking on both the "what" and the "how" of inclusive education. Her work, in particular, on curricular adaptations and universal design of instruction is the inspiration for our own work in differentiated instruction. We must also acknowledge Mayer Shevin for his extraordinary work in the area of behavior supports; he has helped us dream bigger and understand how to work on problems and not on people. Also, we thank Barb Schaffer-Jaffe and all our colleagues at Kruse School who taught us countless lessons about collaboration, consultation, planning, and achieving change.

We are overwhelmingly grateful to our loved ones for supporting us and for allowing us time and space to do the work we love. We apologize for the endless conversations about inclusive schooling during dinner parties, evenings on the town, and at the concerts in the park—we can't help ourselves and you never roll your eyes or change the subject! We appreciate your enthusiasm

for our work more than you know. Thank you Todd, James, Erma, Willa, Rama, and Eden. We also wish to thank Mary, Peggy, Victoria, Vicky, Tim, Sarah, Bob, Katie, and Haley. You all *get it!* Our close friends and colleagues have also been witness to and supportive of our soap box at any given time, therefore, we pay tribute to Sandy, Buck, Kassira, Raul, Tanita, Howard, Tracy, Kevin, Eileen, Aria, and Kaitlynn. We also need to send a great big "gracias amigo" to Paco of New Rebozo. This book would not be possible without the inspiration provided by your wonderful tamales, moles, and ice cream surprises. "Oh My God!"

Finally, we send our gratitude to all at Heinemann and a great big "we are not worthy" to Harvey "Smokey" Daniels who had the idea to put a product like this on the market, allowed us to write it together, and coached us along the way. Thank you Smokey! A huge and continued thank-you also goes to Leigh Peake who supports us in countless ways and Lynne Costa is always a dream to work with. We anticipate and "welcome" many wonderful collaborations in the future.

Differentiating Instruction

A popular mantra of teachers in diverse classrooms is, "If they can't learn the way we teach them, let's teach them the way they learn." This philosophy is at the heart of differentiated instruction, a framework for teaching, learning, and assessment that not only helps us meet the academic needs of our students but also inspires feelings of safety, comfort, excitement, motivation, and satisfaction in our diverse classrooms.

Since the inception of inclusive schooling, scholars and practitioners have used many different terms to describe the type of curriculum, instruction, and assessment that meets the needs of diverse learners. Udvari-Solner (1996) proposes a reflective decision-making model for creating curricular adaptations and responding to all students. Oyler (2001) has used the term *accessible instruction* to describe using democratic practices and developing learning experiences that challenge and support all students. And Tomlinson (1995) has developed a model of "differentiating instruction" to illustrate ways in which teachers can "shake up" what goes on in the classroom and give students "options for taking in information, making sense of ideas, and expressing what they learn" (3).

Having established the "what" of differentiation, we turn to the "why." What is the rationale for using differentiated instruction? First of all, it inspires teachers to reach and teach learners effectively. When we use a wide range of techniques, methods, strategies, and approaches, we reach more students more often. Learners not only perform better in a differentiated classroom but, in a manner of speaking, they "show up" as more confident and capable when we give them a variety of options for learning and demonstrating what they know. Second, differentiated instruction helps us reach the standards. It can be a challenge to cover all of the required content while still keeping students interested and engaged. When we differentiate, however, we are more likely to teach in ways that are both meaningful and memorable. Finally, differentiating helps us keep teaching fresh. It can make our classrooms more cooperative, more collaborative, and perhaps even more joyful. In these pages we offer ten easy ideas for differentiating instruction in your classroom.

1. Ask, Don't Tell

Perhaps the easiest way to differentiate instruction is to frame lessons and units as questions or problems. Consider a typical topic of study—authors. In one classroom, the teacher introduces the topic of "authorship" and tells the students what they will need to know by the end of the unit (e.g., how to research an author). In another classroom, the teacher tells students they will investigate "What is an author?" by studying songwriters, fiction writers, and even graffiti artists. She also tells them that they will be answering a lot of their own questions throughout the unit.

Of the two groups of students, which one is most likely to be highly motivated and appropriately challenged? In our experience, it is typically those students who ask and answer questions, as these learners understand that they are constructing knowledge, not just consuming it. Further, when the unit is presented as a question, the teacher can immediately consider how all students might be able to learn and participate in the unit. "What is an author?" There are *very basic and concrete* and also *very complex* ways to answer that question. During the unit, some students may simply learn that an author is the person who creates a written work. Others may learn (or decide) that the author is the producer of any work (text, piece of art, piece of music) and that authorship may have different meanings to different people. Still others may see the concept in more abstract terms: they may learn about the author as a creator in general and explore how the answer to "What is an author?" may have changed throughout history.

Questions can also help teachers personalize learning for students who have traditionally been excluded from standards-based content. For example, a social studies teacher used provocative questions during a study of the Civil War to engage all her students. Most students could answer "Can you be free if you aren't treated equally?" using information from the class, but at least one student, Amro, a student with cognitive challenges, needed to answer from a more personal point of view. His teacher said, "[He] knew that he was treated differently from his brothers because of his disability and he has a strong opinion about that. If we start with his personal experience, it's a little bit easier for him to make a connection with the Civil War" (Onosko and Jorgensen 1998, 77–78).

2. KEEP THEM ANCHORED

Anchor activities (Feldhusen 1993; Tomlinson 1999) are tasks or assignments that students can work on independently, or at least without teacher support. These activities can be implemented for some period during a class to give teachers time to observe students, engage in individual assessments, or meet with small groups or individual learners.

Anchor activities allow each student to work at a different pace and on different content (if necessary or desired). The only requirements for good anchor activities are that they must be (a) worthy of a student's time, (b) appropriate to the learner's abilities, and (c) easy to "enter" and "exit" so that transitions are short.

Some teachers are reluctant to have students work on tasks or independent activities because they view time that isn't teacher-directed as wasted. When anchor activities are carefully planned, however, nothing could be further from the truth. Independent work that has a purpose gives students opportunities to be *self*-directed, to demonstrate initiative, and to give and get support from peers. Further, anchor activities free teachers from the helm of the classroom, allowing them to use valuable class time for conversations and personalized interactions with learners.

An example of how anchors can buy a teacher quality time with students comes from the eighth-grade English class of Ms. Piehl. In this classroom, anchor activities are used for the first fifteen minutes of each Friday class. The anchor changes from week to week and the directions are posted on the board so that students can begin work immediately upon entering the classroom. The anchor may be silent or partner reading, an ongoing project, or drill-and-practice games. The only rule is that the learners must rely on one another for support. One thing that doesn't change is what the teacher is doing. Ms. Piehl always uses this time to meet with three different students in the class. She has conferences with them about their work and gives them direction on how to improve their skills and become more sophisticated writers. To get the most out of the short blocks of time, Ms. Piehl makes it a rule not to discuss administrative matters, grading, or other non-content-related topics during the conferences. And with this decision she sends a clear message: these meetings are designated for the development of writers!

The reading-writing workshop model developed by Lucy Calkins (1994), Ralph Fletcher and JoAnn Portalupi (2001), Nancie Atwell (1998), and others offers a larger anchoring framework for strong, differentiated instruction in literacy skills. Because this classroom structure is based upon student choice of projects and regular one-on-one conferences with the teacher, it is inherently individualized for all students. Teachers who have already mastered classroom workshop are well on their way to meeting the needs of diverse learners.

3. Partner Up

Another quick and easy way to support a diverse group of learners is through peer tutoring, mentoring, or partnerships. Each of these options helps teachers individualize instruction through personal support. There are a number of useful pair and small group peer-partner models in the instructional literature: peer reading, buddy reading, literature circles, book clubs, co-authors, and more. Here, we want to especially stress three approaches.

Tutors. There are three commonly cited benefits of peer tutoring: academic growth, enhancement of social skills, and improvements in peer relationships (Barone and Barone Schneider 1997; McDonnell et al. 2001; Greenwood et al. 1989). It is a wonder that tutoring relationships are not more common given their low cost and positive outcomes.

One tutoring relationship is peer-to-peer, in which some students have more skill or experience than others and can learn by sharing their expertise. In other instances, teachers may want to use cross-age tutors. Tutors may be recruited from upper grades within the same school or from different buildings (e.g., college students tutoring high school students).

Mentors. Mentors are different from tutors in that they may not teach anything directly. Instead, they serve as coaches or advocates for learners needing direction, inspiration, or advice. Mentors can be adults within the school community (e.g., a psychologist can be a mentor to a student interested in brain research) or outside it (e.g., a local artist might help a student interested in creating an elaborate mural). A mentor can also be an older student. An older child with ADHD might serve as a mentor for a younger child with the same disability, for example.

Study buddies. In her groundbreaking book, *The Dreamkeepers* (1994), Gloria Ladson-Billings highlights the work of a teacher who insists on cooperation and asks students to "buddy up" and support one another from the first day of school:

A lot of times when a student is having a hard time I'll call the buddy to my desk and really give him or her an earful. "Why are you letting your buddy struggle like this? What kind of partner are you? You're supposed to be the helper." Within a couple of months I begin to see them looking out for one another. One student will hesitate before he turns in his paper and will go check to make sure the buddy is doing okay. (72)

Teachers might assign long-term learning partners who review each other's work, study together, teach each other, and support each other. Or they might switch student partners regularly and strategically based on the difficulty, content, and demands of lessons.

4. USE INDIVIDUAL AGENDAS

A learning agenda is a list of projects or activities that must be completed during a specific time, usually during a unit of study. Typically, students work on their agendas independently, asking for support when needed and collaborating with other learners when necessary.

By serving as a visual reminder of the work they have finished and the work they still need to complete, agendas help students develop management and organizational skills. Somewhere on the agenda the teacher can also include a column or a section that indicates any personalized supports, expectations, or reminders for that learner (whether she can use a calculator for computations or should try to use "mental math," for example).

Agenda tasks, of course, vary according to student needs. In one classroom, all students had the same basic agenda for a unit on anatomy ("Make diagrams of each system"; "Read Chapter 7"), but some learners had extra enrichment items ("Interview the school nurse about health occupations"), and one student had an item related to her IEP (Individualized Education Plan) goal of using the telephone ("Call your doctor and ask for information on preventative health"). Similarly, in a unit on the Appalachian Trail, all students received an agenda listing required work, but Paul, a student with dyslexia, had personalized instructions that directed him to available resources, reminded him of unit requirements, and let him know how he would be supported during the unit (see Figure 1).

The Appalachian Trail
Learning Agenda: Paul

Task ✎	Personalized Instructions 🖐	Teacher/Student Initials ✍ (when work is completed satisfactorily)	Teacher Comments ✎	Student Comments ✎
Do a K/W/L chart on the Appalachian Trail with your study partner and put it on our bulletin board.	You must have at least 10 ideas on the chart.			
Complete WebQuest on Appalachian Trail: "5 Million Steps."	Ask your learning buddy for assistance in getting started if you need help.			
Read *Clara and the Hoodoo Man* (Elizabeth Partridge, Puffin Books, 1996).	You must work with Ms. Wix at some point during your reading of the novel. She will ask you to read aloud and to talk about what you are learning from the book.			
Study the AT travel log artifacts, then complete your own modern-day travel log, describing one day on trail. Use the information you have from readings and from brochures collected from state tourism departments.	Use your best punctuation and spelling. Be sure we can clearly read your wonderful account of this journey.			

Figure 1 Example of a Learning Agenda

5. Design Classroom Centers or Stations

Centers or stations are spots in the classroom where small groups of students can work on various tasks simultaneously. Stations can be teacher-led or student-directed and can involve a wide range of activities: web searches or WebQuests, small-group discussions, paper-and-pencil tasks, small projects, independent or partner reading, art or drama exercises, puzzles, interpersonal reflection, mini-lessons, games, chalkboard work, brainstorming, DVD viewing, and observations or examinations of processes or materials.

For example, learners in a secondary school math class might rotate through five stations with specific goals and outcomes:

- Working with the teacher to learn about probability
- Solving probability problems from the textbook
- Generating a list of real-world applications for probability
- Working on a new computer program with a small group
- Completing a review worksheet from the last unit

All students might be expected to work at all stations, or the teacher might personalize the lesson by having some students work at only some of the stations or by differentiating tasks at the stations so that some students complete more complex problems or tasks than others.

According to Tomlinson (1999), centers should focus on important learning goals; contain materials that help individual students reach those goals; use activities geared to a wide range of reading levels, learning profiles, and student interests; provide clear directions; include instructions about what students should do when they complete the work; and include a record-keeping system to monitor what students do at the center and how well they do it.

Centers or station teaching and inclusive education are a perfect fit, because centers allow teachers to work with individual students or small groups of learners without removing them from the classroom. For example, a general educator can oversee the entire class as the students move through the rotations, while a special educator checks in with those learners needing alternative questions, materials, or instruction. In addition, this format involves interactive work and allows students to socialize, collaborate, and learn from one another.

6. Assign Projects

Project-based instruction is especially appropriate for students with diverse learning profiles because:

- Many student needs and learning styles can be addressed.
- There are increased opportunities for peer relationships and support.
- Students can work at their own pace.
- Multiple skills and disciplines can be incorporated.

Projects are also ideal for students who enjoy working independently or who thrive when given opportunities to immerse themselves in one topic. Donna Williams (1992), a very gifted author and poet with autism, found that she could be academically successful when a favorite teacher believed in her abilities and let her pursue a topic of special interest—the United States civil rights movement—in depth:

> I had gone through every book I could find on the topic, cutting out pictures and drawing illustrations over my written pages, as I had always done, to capture the feel of what I wanted to write about. The other students had given her projects spanning an average of about three pages in length. I proudly gave her my special project of twenty-six pages, illustrations, and drawings. She gave me an A. (81)

When using projects, teachers should set clear timelines, teach students how to chart their own progress and develop progress reports, and help students produce a final product or products. In addition, steering students away from merely copying and collating material and toward activities that will inspire higher-order thinking and meaningful engagement will result in more inspired projects and more motivated students. You might ask learners to design a model, compare ideas, create a product, or produce a mural instead of merely submitting a report. For example, when four seventh graders were studying their school district's recycling program, their teacher, Mr. Ochoa, suggested they summarize the opinions of two experts, interview two school employees, and invent a model policy to present to the school board.

Other ideas for project-based instruction include:

- Developing a curriculum to teach other students about something
- Creating art (e.g., for the community, for the school)
- Proposing legislation
- Inventing a product
- Writing and producing a movie
- Launching a website based on class content

7. Create Choose-and-Learn Boxes

In most instances, differentiation is carefully crafted by the classroom teacher or by a teaching team. But sometimes educators find they must meet the needs of diverse learners on the spot. In these situations, "Choose-and-Learn Boxes," a curricular adaptation we developed for use in K–12 classrooms, can fill that need.

Choose-and-learn boxes are simply some kind of container (e.g., shoe box, milk crate) filled with curriculum-related (and, if possible, standards-linked) materials that paraprofessionals, general educators, and special educators can use as a substitute for a planned activity, a filler for times when an activity has not been appropriately planned, or a fidget or stay-put support for a learner needing something to manipulate during a difficult time. For instance, one middle school math teacher, Mr. Fischer, often gave very extensive explanations of mathematical concepts, and when he did, J.C., a student with significant learning disabilities, would get very anxious and jumpy and would often begin bothering his classmates, muttering under his breath, or even asking the teacher when he would "be done talking!" When Mr. Fisher sensed the lecture was becoming too intense for J.C., he directed his student to use materials from the classroom choose-and-learn box until it was time to begin the assignment with his cooperative math group. J.C. might grab a math-related game or puzzle or simply take a mini-chalkboard out so he could continue following the classroom presentation by using different materials to take notes or participate.

A sixth-grade mathematics choose-and-learn box might include fraction bars, calculators, an adding machine, various worksheets, puzzles, a wipe-off board/mini-chalkboard, brain teaser books, and compact discs of math-related music (e.g., division rap). A high school U.S. history choose-and-learn box might include flashcards or playing cards featuring famous Americans, crossword puzzles or word finds with historical themes, issues of *Newsweek* or *National Geographic* magazine, a handheld computer trivia game, brochures and pamphlets of American landmarks, and small desktop jigsaw puzzles with historical themes (e.g., Rosie the Riveter). A second-grade spelling choose-and-learn box might include foam letters, stencils, magnetic words, flashcards, finger paint, a hand-held label maker, and alphabet stickers or stamps.

Of course, these activities and materials should *never* be the centerpiece of any student's educational program. Choose-and-learn activities should be used supportively in instructional emergencies to keep learners connected to course content and to prevent periods of frustration and disconnection. While these materials might be used primarily for students with disabilities or learning differences, some teachers may want to allow any student to access them during certain parts of the daily lesson or when they finish assigned work.

Giving students opportunities to work with a wide range of materials allows the teacher to observe student choices and interactions and may inspire ideas for future lessons, curricular adaptations, and learning supports. In this way, the boxes serve as a planning tool for teachers and as a way for learners to identify what they need to be successful.

8. "Shake Up" Adult Roles and Responsibilities

Consider this scenario: Ms. Rincon is a paraeducator in an inclusive sixth-grade classroom. It is her responsibility to make sure that two students with learning disabilities and one learner with emotional disabilities stay on task. She listens while Ms. Goddard, the classroom teacher, provides instruction. When Ms. Goddard gives students time to work on their own, Ms. Rincon splits her time among the three students to whom she is assigned, moving from one desk to the next to provide support. If the three students are all working efficiently, Ms. Rincon sits next to one of them and supervises that student's work.

While on the surface, these roles may appear appropriate, two critical questions lead us to consider how a shift in roles and responsibilities can inspire more differentiation in the classroom: *How can Ms. Rincon's talents be used to support a wider range of learners? How can Ms. Goddard collaborate with Ms. Rincon to teach more effectively?*

Here's a revised scenario that answers these questions. Ms. Rincon has many different responsibilities. During whole-class instruction, she often teaches alongside Ms. Goddard. Since she does not know the content very well, she contributes by writing down key points or by taking "picture" notes on the chalkboard; this helps boost the comprehension of students who profit from both hearing and seeing the content. When it is time to read aloud to the students or to have them read aloud, Ms. Rincon and Ms. Goddard each work with a small group so individual learners have more opportunities to share. When students are working on their own or in small groups, Ms. Rincon checks on those with identified needs before moving on to question, support, and direct other learners in the classroom. If no one in particular needs help, she moves from student to student and asks each an enrichment question that Ms. Goddard has created.

In order to make these types of changes, begin by assessing what the adults in your building do and do not do on an average day. Then make some changes in roles and responsibilities so that all adults can provide better and more purposeful support and instruction to all learners (see the accompanying book *Collaboration and Teaming in the Inclusive Classroom* for more ideas).

9. Plan to Overlap

In inclusive classrooms, students with unique learning profiles, including those with disabilities and those with identified gifts, do not need to learn the same curriculum, use the same materials, or have the same goals as their classmates. They should, however, be exposed to standards-based content and learn in meaningful ways alongside their peers.

With an overlapping curriculum, students needing more support or enrichment can work on objectives that are different from the ones their peers are working on but still connected to classroom work. For example, during a series of lessons on Central America, a student who already knew a lot about geography and politics created a website that connected students to classrooms in that region. A student with cognitive disabilities wrote a short letter to a student pen pal living in Honduras, thus having an opportunity to learn about the nation through a peer, understand how to use a word processing program, and practice using new vocabulary words. (The completed correspondence was then used as a teaching and learning tool for the rest of the class.) Other examples are:

- During a "family and consumer education" sewing lesson, a student worked on the math skill of one-to-one correspondence by distributing spools of thread and bolts of fabric to members of her group. She also worked with a partner to iron finished products and package them for sale in the school store.

- While students in a third-grade math class were learning about fractions, a student with developmental disabilities made cookies with a few peers. Some students read the recipe (complete with several fractions) and found the appropriate measuring tools, while others did the actual scooping, stirring, and baking.

- During an English lesson on the use of symbolism in John Steinbeck's *Grapes of Wrath*, a student with a traumatic brain injury listened to the presentation while she worked with a team to create props for skits related to the novel. Through this activity the young woman addressed a vocational goal of learning about theater-related jobs.

Overlapping can be a useful tool but should be used with caution. In today's standards-based climate, all students should be given as many opportunities as possible to learn general education content and meet the corresponding goals. Overlapping should only be used when the content is very difficult to adapt successfully, when a student is not expected to access some aspect of the curriculum, and/or when the chosen mode of instruction is not conducive to the student's learning style and another adaptation cannot be made.

10. INTEGRATE THE IEP

Some students in inclusive classrooms have Individualized Education Plans (IEPs). An IEP is developed by a collaborative team of professionals and the student's family to pinpoint what skills and competencies are most appropriate for this student to learn and practice during a school day.

Traditionally, the IEP was used as a guide for curriculum development. That is, teachers created entire lesson plans based solely on IEP objectives: if a student had a goal related to counting coins, a daily lesson might revolve around this skill. More recently, teachers interested in providing all students with a more rigorous education have stopped creating lessons or activities around single objectives and instead have looked for ways to address objectives throughout the day within the standards-based lessons taught in general education classrooms. This way, targeted objectives are not taught once a day during a short lesson but are highlighted, addressed, and assessed throughout the school day, week, and year. To use the coin counting goal as an example, the teacher of that student might address coin counting during times in the day when it would be natural to work with money (e.g., in math class, when paying for lunch, when purchasing milk during the morning break) instead of teaching the skill in isolation.

The IEP matrix (see Figure 2) makes this type of planning easier and more systematic. Teachers can scan the goals and the student's schedule at the same time and consider where and how the two might intersect. Consider, for instance, how Ms. Wendt, a fifth-grade teacher, used an IEP matrix to differentiate a science unit and, in particular, to meet the needs of Joseph, a student with cognitive disabilities. One of Joseph's IEP objectives was to learn to use a calculator. To give him extra practice beyond the math hour, Ms. Wendt looked at the IEP matrix and located two additional places to practice the skill: she added a math problem to all her science units (Joseph had

Opportunities to Address IEP Goals: Joseph

Daily Classes/ Activities	IEP Objectives				
	J. will use a capital letter at the beginning of each sentence and an appropriate ending mark.	J. will write a complete sentence without prompts or cues.	J. will independently operate a calculator.	J. will ask for assistance from his general educator or a peer when he cannot complete his work independently.	J. will engage in a preferred leisure activity for 10 minutes at a time.
recess & locker				X	X
language arts	X	X		X	
social studies	X	X		X	
music	X	X		X	X
lunch					X
science	X	X	X	X	
math		X	X	X	

Figure 2 An Example of an IEP Matrix

to calculate how many pounds of paper the fifth graders were recycling during the ecology unit) and she gave a few students (Joseph among them) opportunities to calculate on-base percentages and other statistics during baseball games at recess.

Common Questions

What about the standards? Is it possible to differentiate when I have to meet high standards and prepare my students for high-stakes tests?

While some teachers may be apprehensive about giving up traditional instructional practices in this climate of high-stakes testing, using differentiated instruction and diverse teaching strategies can actually enhance learning for many students (Udvari-Solner 1996). Teachers should use the standards as curricular goals but employ multilevel and student-centered techniques to help learners reach those goals.

In other words, teachers need not respond to the standards movement *by standardizing teaching and learning.* No student should be expected to know and do *exactly* the same things as her or his same-age peers at the end of a school year. The standards must be viewed as flexible. This orientation provides different students in the same classroom with opportunities to work on a range of concepts and skills, based on individual abilities, needs, and interests (Reigeluth 1997). For example, students may meet the standard "Explain to others how to solve a numerical problem" in dozens of different ways. Some may use calculators or manipulatives to show understanding, others may explain in a written paragraph, still others may best express their knowledge by designing flowcharts. In addition, the numerical problem they explain may range in complexity from describing the process for adding single digits to designing and explaining binomial equations.

How can I differentiate for a student with more significant disabilities?
Students with disabilities do not need to "keep up" with students without disabilities in order to be educated in inclusive classrooms; they do not need to engage in the curriculum in the same way as students without disabilities; and they do not need to practice the same skills as students without disabilities. In classrooms that use differentiated instruction, all students can get what they need while working together and learning side by side. Using tools that have been outlined in this book, teachers can personalize instruction while challenging and supporting all students.

For instance, a middle school social studies class is studying American immigration in the early 1900s. During the unit, students pretend that they are newcomers arriving in America. Each student is required to research the life of a real immigrant using primary sources and present information about this person during the simulation. Eve, a student with significant disabilities, participates in these activities even though she is not able to communicate reliably and is just beginning to read. To begin, Eve works with a peer (see Partner Up, p. 6) and a speech and language therapist to create a document that will be used as a passport of sorts. She listens to her partner read a bit about "Mary Malone" and then chooses three pieces of information from five sentence strips to paste on her "immigration papers."

At "Ellis Island," students are working at stations (see Design Classroom Centers or Stations, p. 10) that represent activities most newcomers engaged in as they arrived in New York (e.g., medical examinations, legal interviews). Eve, acting as the Commissioner of Immigration at one of the stations, asks each of her classmates questions about their lives and their journey ("Who are you and why did you come to America?") using her augmentative communication device (a Dynamo®). Having this special role gives Eve opportunities to practice using the device while still keeping connected to the content (see Plan to Overlap, p. 18). This activity also helps her address her IEP goal of "using her augmentative communication device to ask and answer content-based questions" (see Integrate the IEP, p. 20).

As you can see from the example, many of the strategies we have shared throughout this book can be used simultaneously, and students with disabilities can participate in general education without engaging in the same ways and without demonstrating the same skills and abilities others in the class may have.

I have been teaching for twenty years and now they are telling me I have to differentiate and include and adapt and change my instruction. I don't feel I have the time, support, or patience to learn a new way to teach. How can I learn these new techniques now?

The first time general education teachers find a student with a disability (or one identified as needing enrichment) on their class list, they may feel unprepared to support that learner. Teachers often feel incapable of providing personalized education, and they commonly worry about not being trained in techniques related to special education, ESL (English as a Second Language), bilingual, or gifted education. In other words, many educators believe that they need specialized strategies to teach diverse learners.

While it can certainly be beneficial at times to know about particular differences before teaching students with those differences, teachers can be incredibly effective simply by being accepting, looking for strengths in learners, providing personal attention when necessary, and allowing for individuality in the ways students approach tasks and complete classroom work. That is, teachers often practice differentiated instruction and inclusive pedagogy just by engaging in good teaching. For instance:

- When a teacher allows students different ways to express their understanding of a concept (taking a written test, designing a piece of art, giving a speech), she is differentiating instruction.

- When a teacher presents a range of materials to teach a new idea (models, visuals, encyclopedias, interactive software), he is differentiating instruction.

- When a teacher makes informed decisions about grouping students for instruction, she is differentiating instruction.

- When a teacher gives students opportunities to support and teach one another, he is differentiating instruction.

- When a teacher shows students how to complete an assignment by demonstrating it and by providing the directions in writing, she is differentiating instruction.

In other words, teachers who understand difference and respond to learners as individuals are most likely differentiating instruction even if they do not use that term to describe what they do. For most of us, effectively teaching diverse learners in the general education classroom will simply involve expanding the strategies and approaches we already use.

References

Recommended Books

Chapman, C., and R. Cook. 2004. *Differentiated Assessment Strategies: One Tool Doesn't Fit All*. Thousand Oaks, CA: Corwin. If we differentiate instruction, we will need to differentiate assessment. These authors offer options for measuring, discussing, and documenting student progress.

Conklin, W. 2006. *Instructional Strategies for Differentiated Learning*. Huntington Beach, CA: Shell Educational. A handful of key strategies are featured in this small, user-friendly guide.

Frey, N., D. Fisher, and K. Moore. 2005. *Designing Responsive Curriculum: Planning Lessons That Work*. Lanham, MD: Rowman & Littlefield. This book is built around classroom lessons, providing the "how-to" component of instruction design for those in diverse, inclusive classrooms.

Gregory, G. (2005). *Differentiating Instruction with Style: Aligning Teacher and Learner Intelligences for Maximum Achievement*. Thousand Oaks, CA: Corwin. In this volume, Gregory takes a unique look at the "how" of differentiation by exploring student learning styles and intelligences.

Harmin, M., and M. Toth. 2006. *Inspiring Active Learning: A Complete Handbook for Today's Teachers*. Alexandria, VA: Association for Supervision and Curriculum Development (ASCD). These activities can be used in either elementary or secondary schools and will transform your teaching!

Janney, R., and M. E. Snell. 2000. *Modifying Schoolwork*. Baltimore, MD: Paul H. Brookes. This small but mighty resource provides suggestions for adapting tests, expanding teaching strategies, and creating supplemental materials.

Lewis, B. 1995. *The Kids' Guide to Service Projects*. Minneapolis, MN: Free Spirit. While service learning is not often referred to in the differentiation literature, we find it is one of the most meaningful ways to teach to all.

Silberman, M. 1996. *Active Learning: 101 Strategies to Teach Any Subject*. Boston: Allyn and Bacon. This rich, teacher-friendly resource is as appropriate for the kindergarten teacher as it is for the college professor.

Silver, D. 1999. *Drumming to the Beat of a Different Marcher: Finding the Rhythm for Teaching a Differentiated Classroom*. Nashville, TN: Incentive. This is a worthwhile read that will inspire and challenge those interested in building a classroom community and responding to the uniqueness in all learners.

Tomlinson, C. A. 2002. *How to Differentiate in a Mixed-ability Classroom*. Alexandria, VA: Association for Supervision and Curriculum Development (ASCD). To collect even more strategies for the differentiated classroom, look no further than this popular book. Strategies featured include "sidebar" investigations, entry points, and portfolios.

———. 2003. *Fulfilling the Promise of the Differentiated Classroom: Strategies and Tools for Responsive Teaching*. Alexandria, VA: Association for Supervision and Curriculum Development (ASCD). Tomlinson takes us to the next level of differentiated curriculum and instruction by exploring achievement (what it is and how to get there).

Recommended Websites

The Access Center: www.k8accesscenter.org/default.asp

The Access Center is a national technical assistance (TA) center funded by the U.S. Department of Education's Office of Special Education Programs. Their mission is to improve educational outcomes for elementary and middle students with disabilities.

Carol Ann Tomlinson's website: www.caroltomlinson.com

No other name is associated more directly with differentiated instruction than Carol Ann Tomlinson. Her website contains a list of her publications, links to other great websites (including some constructed by her college students), and additional resources.

CAST: www.cast.org/pd/index.html

The Center for Applied Special Technology is a nonprofit organization that works to expand learning opportunities for all, especially those with disabilities, through the development of innovative, technology-based educational resources and strategies.

Paula Kluth's Home Page: www.paulakluth.com

> Paula's website includes dozens of articles on inclusive school-
> ing, literacy in diverse classrooms, and differentiating instruction.
> Topics addressed include adapting textbooks, differentiating
> through service learning, and curriculum overlapping.

TeachersFirst: www.teachersfirst.com

> The Teachers First website offers suggestions of techniques for
> adapting curriculum for learners who have disabilities. It pro-
> vides a good resource of strategies for effectively teaching
> diverse learners of all ages.

Works Cited

Barone, D., and R. Barone Schneider. 1997. "Cross-age Tutoring."
Childhood Education 73: 136–43.

Feldhusen, H. J. 1993. "Individualized Teaching of the Gifted in Regular Classrooms." In *Critical Issues in Gifted Education: Programs for
the Gifted in Regular Classrooms,* ed. C. J. Maker, 263–73. Austin,
TX: PRO-ED.

Greenwood, C. R., J. C. Delquardi, and R. V. Hall. 1989. "Longitudi-
nal Effects of Classwide Peer Tutoring. *Journal of Educational Psychology* 81: 371–83.

Ladson-Billings, G. 1994. *The Dreamkeepers.* San Francisco: Jossey-
Bass.

McDonnell, J., C. Mathot-Buckner, N. Thorson, and S. Fister. 2001.
"Supporting the Inclusion of Students with Moderate and Severe
Disabilities in Junior High School General Education Classes: The
Effects of Classwide Peer Tutoring, Multi-element Curriculum, and
Accommodations." *Education and Treatment of Children* 24: 141–60.

Onosko, J., and C. Jorgensen. 1998. "Unit and Lesson Planning in the
Inclusive Classroom: Maximizing Learning Opportunities for All
Students. In *Restructuring High Schools for All Students,* ed. C. Jor-
gensen, 71–105. Baltimore, MD: Paul H. Brookes.

Reigeluth, C. M. 1997. "Educational Standards: To Standardize or to
Customize Learning? *Phi Delta Kappan* 79: 202–6.

Tomlinson, C. A. 1999. *The Differentiated Classroom: Responding to the
Needs of All Learners.* Alexandria, VA: Association for Supervision
and Curriculum Development (ASCD).

———. 2001. *How to Differentiate Instruction in a Mixed-ability Classroom,* Alexandria, VA: Association for Supervision and Curriculum
Development (ASCD).

Udvari-Solner, A. 1996. "Examining Teacher Thinking: Constructing
a Process to Design Curricular Adaptations. *Remedial and Special
Education* 17: 245–54.

You're Welcome

Positive

& Peaceful

Behavior

Supports

for the

Inclusive

Classroom

Patrick Schwarz
& Paula Kluth

HEINEMANN
Portsmouth, NH

To our fathers, Jimmy and Joseph,
For giving us the belief that doing good things
for people matters most.

Heinemann
A division of Reed Elsevier Inc.
361 Hanover Street
Portsmouth, NH 03801–3912
www.heinemann.com

Offices and agents throughout the world

© 2007 by Patrick Schwarz and Paula Kluth

Library of Congress Cataloging-in-Publication Data
Schwarz, Patrick.
   You're welcome : 30 innovative ideas for the inclusive classroom / Patrick Schwarz
and Paula Kluth.
      p. cm.
   Includes bibliographical references.
   ISBN-13: 978-0-325-01204-9
   ISBN-10: 0-325-01204-0
   1. Individualized instruction—United States. 2. Inclusive education—United States.
3. Group work in education—United States. 4. Multicultural education—United
States. I. Kluth, Paula. II. Title.

LB1031.S39 2007
371.9'046—dc22   2007016386

Editor: Harvey Daniels
Production: Lynne Costa
Cover design: Joni Doherty Design
Cover illustration: © Kevin Tolman/Photodisc/GettyImages
Typesetter: Kim Arney
Manufacturing: Louise Richardson

Printed in the United States of America on acid-free paper
11   10   09   08   07   CG   1   2   3   4   5

Contents

Acknowledgments

We are grateful to the many people who supported us to complete this project. Above all, we are indebted to the students with *possibilities* who have challenged us, taught us, and welcomed us into their lives over the years. We have been educated by many wonderful young people including Paul, Jason, Franklin, Tim, Mark, Jamie, Libby, Susan, Joe, Bob, Adam, Matt, John, Aaron, Andrew, and Bob.

The work of colleagues has also inspired this project, especially that of our dear colleague and friend, Alice Udvari-Solner. She has been a teacher to us for many years and constantly pushes our thinking on both the "what" and the "how" of inclusive education. Her work, in particular, on curricular adaptations and universal design of instruction is the inspiration for our own work in differentiated instruction. We must also acknowledge Mayer Shevin for his extraordinary work in the area of behavior supports; he has helped us dream bigger and understand how to work on problems and not on people. Also, we thank Barb Schaffer-Jaffe and all our colleagues at Kruse School who taught us countless lessons about collaboration, consultation, planning, and achieving change.

We are overwhelmingly grateful to our loved ones for supporting us and for allowing us time and space to do the work we love. We apologize for the endless conversations about inclusive schooling during dinner parties, evenings on the town, and at the concerts in the park—we can't help ourselves and you never roll your eyes or change the subject! We appreciate your enthusiasm

for our work more than you know. Thank you Todd, James, Erma, Willa, Rama, and Eden. We also wish to thank Mary, Peggy, Victoria, Vicky, Tim, Sarah, Bob, Katie, and Haley. You all *get it!* Our close friends and colleagues have also been witness to and supportive of our soap box at any given time, therefore, we pay tribute to Sandy, Buck, Kassira, Raul, Tanita, Howard, Tracy, Kevin, Eileen, Aria, and Kaitlynn. We also need to send a great big "gracias amigo" to Paco of New Rebozo. This book would not be possible without the inspiration provided by your wonderful tamales, moles, and ice cream surprises. "Oh My God!"

Finally, we send our gratitude to all at Heinemann and a great big "we are not worthy" to Harvey "Smokey" Daniels who had the idea to put a product like this on the market, allowed us to write it together, and coached us along the way. Thank you Smokey! A huge and continued thank-you also goes to Leigh Peake who supports us in countless ways and Lynne Costa is always a dream to work with. We anticipate and "welcome" many wonderful collaborations in the future.

Positive and Peaceful Behavior Supports

The notion of "supporting behavior" is tricky. In the literature, in teacher preparation materials, and in daily language, educators often use words and phrases that seem to suggest that behavior occurs in a vacuum—or worse, that it is located inside the student. In reality, behavior cannot be set apart from curriculum, instruction, teaching and learning, relationships, school culture, issues of community, and hundreds of other factors.

Because behavior is so complex, we will discuss it as a phenomenon that is *interpreted*: all behavior is perceived differently by different individuals, including the person who is demonstrating it. A teacher may see a student's doodling as off task, while that learner may be drawing as a way to maintain appropriate behavior (remain seated and connected to the class discussion). All behavior is also contextual: it occurs under circumstances, in settings, and with people. Students generally seen as "behavior problems" may be very calm, focused, and "appropriate" with certain teachers and in certain environments. In other words, behavior doesn't "live" inside students; it often erupts, however, when students don't have the support they need.

In our work with teachers and school leaders we therefore focus on creating schools that are responsive, respectful, and safe as much as or more than we do on addressing challenging behavior. The most important reason to study how school culture, climate, and teaching strategies can change (instead of considering only how a student might do so) is that changing people is hard work but changing the environment, our response to a situation, or our instructional materials can be quite simple. The other reason is that when we make changes to our teaching, curriculum, supports, expectations, or learning environment for one student, many other learners benefit.

One last point: although it is possible to have a school that is responsive, respectful, and safe but not inclusive, it is, by definition, impossible to have an inclusive school that is not responsive, respectful, and safe.

1. Ask Different Questions

We once consulted with a team that was supporting Dakota, a student identified as having emotional disabilities. They told us his behavior was getting worse in spite of everything they had tried, including rewards, punishments, removal from certain environments, even meetings with both the principal and a local police officer. They wanted to know,

> *How can we get him to "behave" and complete his work?*
>
> *How can we get him to respect adults and school property?*
>
> *How can we get him to comply with directions and requests?*
>
> *What kind of consequence might be effective in motivating him to change his behavior?*
>
> *What kind of reinforcement might be effective in motivating him to change his behavior?*

When we observed the young man, he did indeed exhibit challenges. While receiving instruction in his self-contained classroom, he experienced a "melt down" every time other students left to attend general education classes. He threw materials off his desk, refused to do work, and sometimes dropped to the floor and refused to get up. On one occasion, he had even broken a classroom window. These episodes happened at different times during the day but his distress was most severe when all the other students left for lunch and he had to remain behind to eat with a paraeducator.

In studying Dakota's activities and experiences, we found that his day was unusually isolating, almost completely void of social interaction. He received most of his instruction alone or with one other peer. His curriculum consisted of a lot of drill-and-skill and paper-and-pencil exercises and he seldom, if ever, experienced moments of fun and playfulness. The team defended his placement on the grounds that "he can be a handful and we can control him better in isolation."

This approach is far too common. When supporting students with behavior challenges, we often encourage compliance over self-advocacy and teach students to act as others do instead of helping them identify individual needs. In addition, we educators spend a lot of time getting students to do what we want them to do without considering what it is we are expecting, why we are expecting it, or if it is reasonable and appropriate to expect it.

It is so critical to keep in mind how complex behavior change is and to realize that just because we can get a student to do something doesn't always mean we should! In many cases, we need to, instead, ask new questions and gather more information about the behavior and its function. For instance, if a student resists a task it might be helpful to know why. Is the task too difficult? Is the student bored? Are the directions clear? If a student gets out of his seat constantly, we might want to explore when he does it and for what purpose. Is he avoiding something? Does he need something? Does he do it all the time or just during certain activities? Is the behavior helpful in some way? Does he intend to be disruptive?

In Dakota's situation, the team might have fared better had they taken up this very approach and focused on a different set of questions. Instead of only developing strategies that would get Dakota to "do his work," the team might have considered the following questions:

- What is he trying to communicate with his behavior?
- Does he feel comfortable? Safe? Valued? Empowered?
- Is his curriculum appropriately challenging? Motivating? Interesting?
- Is the instruction responsive?
- Is the classroom environment conducive to learning?
- Does he have the proper supports or adaptations?
- How can we help him become more connected to others?
- How can we help him experience more happiness and joy at school?

2. EVALUATE THE "PROBLEM"

Often when a student exhibits unusual or challenging behavior, special education professionals work to "extinguish" the behavior. While it is certainly appropriate to help students change behavior that may hurt themselves or others, in other instances it is often more appropriate to accept the behavior and work to understand it—in other words, to change our attitude. For example, Marcus was a student with autism who played drums in the school band. He was a skilled musician and could easily follow as Mr. England, his band teacher, conducted, but he would repeat in a booming voice every direction given (e.g., "Get your instruments ready!") and the name of every song Mr. England asked the band to play. This repetitive speech (*echolalia*), involuntary in Marcus's case, didn't appear to bother the band members but it upset Mr. England. Therefore, he, Marcus, some of the band members, and a few of Marcus's support staff met to try to solve the problem.

The group proposed these options:

- Mr. England could ignore the utterances.
- Mr. England could give gestural instead of verbal cues.
- Mr. England could ask Marcus to "co-introduce" the songs.
- Mr. England could have all the band members shout out the names of songs.
- Students could try cuing Marcus to speak more softly (touch him on the shoulder, for example).

Unfortunately, Mr. England wouldn't try any of these ideas. Band practice became very frustrating for Mr. England and for Marcus, and eventually the young man left the band.

Who has a problem in this scenario? While Marcus was embarrassed by his outbursts, he found that he had little control over them. He found that his echolalia often "acted up" when he was in new situations and, ironically, when he was under stress.

Patricia Howlin (1998) describes a similar scenario in her account of Guy, a young man with learning disabilities who often disrupted lessons by arriving late to his classes and noisily scrounging for materials. When Guy's support staff suggested simply that he be allowed to have a desk stocked with necessary materials in all of his classrooms, making class-to-class transitions easier, a few teachers resisted:

> Some teachers were happy to implement these suggestions and in their classes Guy's behavior improved rapidly. Others refused to change long-established teaching practices and in these classes his behavior remained highly disruptive and erratic. (p. 244)

Both of these stories highlight the fact that some challenges have relatively simple solutions. Before we tackle difficulties, we should first ask:

- Is this behavior really a problem?
- If so, is the behavior a problem for the student, the staff, or both?
- Can we solve the problem by changing our attitude or approach—can we be more open, understanding, or creative?

3. Build a Relationship

Supporting a person exhibiting difficult behavior begins when we make a commitment to *know* the person. Sadly, people who intervene to stop someone from engaging in difficult behavior often do not know the individual in any meaningful sense. Instead, they see the person as someone (read, some*thing*) that needs to be fixed or modified.

As David Pitonyak (2005) points out, "The first step in supporting a person with difficult behaviors almost seems too obvious to state: *get to know the person!*" Creative teachers often make a point of spending personal time with struggling students and getting to know them, their families, their needs, and their abilities. Leanne Johnson (1998), for example, the teacher made famous in the popular film *Dangerous Minds*, often asked her students to have lunch with her to discuss concerns and explore how they could work more collaboratively in the classroom.

Herb Lovett (1996) has stressed that *making connections* with students is central to any other work we do related to behavioral support. He highlighted the importance of showing our feelings and our very humanity:

> A positive approach [to behavior issues] invites people to enter into the same sort of relationship that most of us have and treasure: ongoing, with mutual affection and regard. In such relationships, we all make mistakes, are all in some ways inadequate, and yet it is not the level of success that makes the relationship so satisfying to the people involved: it is the ongoing commitment. In the context of relationships, the success and failure of our work becomes harder to assess because the key elements no longer involve simply quantity but the more complex issues of quality. We professionals have routinely overlooked the significance of relationships. (137)

Gallagher (1997) writes about one teacher who took the charge of showing concern and making teacher-to-student connections so seriously that she began greeting students at the door every day and complimenting them using descriptors such as *worthy, valuable,* and *on the edge of greatness.* Other ways to express support and build relationships include:

- Periodically meeting one-on-one with students to learn about their individual abilities, needs, and concerns
- Exchanging letters or emails with students, either formally (as part of a classroom assignment) or informally (dialogue about favorite books, television programs)
- Building getting-to-know-you content into curriculum and instruction (e.g., having students write a two-page autobiography for English class or make a presentation on their family history in social studies).

4. Ask "How's Your Health?"

Trina lived in a group home, did not have a job, and had little contact with people outside her apartment. When we met her, she had a lot of "behavior issues." She refused to get out of bed in the morning, and when people tried to help her do so, she kicked and bit. While giving Trina a routine physical, her doctor asked about the bruises on her arms. Her support team explained the daily struggle. The doctor asked several questions and recommended that Trina see a psychologist, who diagnosed her with clinical depression. As a result, the support team made many changes in her schedule, activities, and diet. She also began to see a counselor regularly. Once these changes had been implemented, her challenging behavior disappeared. One of the team members mused, "I thought she was just difficult. I didn't think Trina *could* get depressed!"

People with disabilities are vulnerable to the same illnesses, health risks, and psychiatric conditions as the general population. Part of helping people with challenging behavior is recognizing this and creating supports that are more humanitarian, holistic, and responsive. Too often, those supporting students with disabilities understand behavior as something intentional and within the person's control. In some cases, the behavior is neither. And even when it is intentional, the individual may be using behavior to communicate a need (e.g., comfort).

Another reason medical problems are overlooked in this population is communication difficulties. Some students may not be able to report symptoms because they are not able to speak. Others may be able to speak but may lack necessary language skills. Still others may have problems perceiving the nature of their condition. For instance, students with some conditions may not experience pain in the way most people do. A student we know with autism reports that paper cuts feel more uncomfortable to him than ear infections.

For all these reasons, teachers need to ask several essential questions related to physiology as they explore student difficulties:

- Are basic needs being met (e.g., nutrition)?
- Might this person need to see her or his doctor?
- Could the behavior be related to medications?
- Could the person be in pain?
- Could the person be suffering from a hidden problem (e.g., mental illness)?

5. Learn to Read Behavior "Messages"

Difficult behavior is often a "message" that can tell us important things about a person's quality of life. Indeed, *the most difficult behavior often results from an unmet need.*

While some behavior might simply be a symptom of a particular disability (e.g., the swearing done by a person with Tourette's syndrome), other behavior can convey any of the following messages:

- "I'm lonely."
- "I'm depressed."
- "I'm bored."
- "I'm angry."
- "I'm hurt."
- "I'm frustrated."
- "I'm confused."
- "I'm uncomfortable."
- "I'm sick."
- "I'm scared."
- "I'm in pain."
- "I have no power."
- "I don't feel safe."
- "I need help."
- "I need attention."
- "I don't think you care about me."
- "I can't do what you are asking me to."
- "I don't understand what you are asking me to do."

When we view behavior as a message, we will focus on unraveling what the individual is trying to convey and how we can respond to their communication rather than on how we can change the person or get them to behave as we want them to.

Sometimes it may be difficult for students to explain their behavior because they lack communication skills, are immature, aren't self-confident, or are inexperienced. In that case, the teacher must "decode" the message. For example, Todd, a student with Down syndrome, would, at times, jump up from his seat and run out of the classroom (and, occasionally, out of the school). Certain educators in the school were alarmed by these actions and viewed this behavior as evidence that Todd was not ready for an inclusive placement. His support team felt the problem was one that should be solved not by segregating Todd but by talking to him, giving him information, encouraging him, and making guesses about the purpose, intention, or message of their student's behaviors. They noticed that Todd engaged in most of these behaviors at the end of the school day or anytime he was made to sit down for long periods of time and keep quiet. By escaping the classroom, he seemed to be communicating, "Get me out of here. I can't keep still anymore."

The team, therefore, taught Todd to say, "I need a break," whenever he was uncomfortable. At first, Todd indicated that he needed a break quite often. The team honored each of these requests by immediately ushering Todd out of the room and walking a few laps around the hallway with him (or out of the school and around the block if he was feeling especially frustrated). They also worked to reduce his anxiety in the classroom by giving him a more comfortable chair, a notepad to doodle on, and several classroom jobs that allowed him to move around throughout the day. In addition, he was given permission to pace in the back of the room when he was getting antsy. Over time, all of these supports helped Todd become more at ease in his inclusive classroom. His requests for a break became much less frequent and he became more effective at communicating his needs to teachers and peers alike.

6. Teach Self-Management

Some students act as they do because they do not have certain skills or competencies. All students, but particularly those who have unusually stressful lives (e.g., those without much family support), may need skills that help them cope with challenges and calm down in difficult moments. Three essential skills are relaxation, role playing, and visualization. All contribute to a greater understanding of how to support oneself effectively.

Relaxation. Progressive relaxation (a technique appropriate for any student) involves tensing and releasing various muscles of the body from the head to the toes, or the toes to the head (Cautela and Groden 1978). Once we teach students the steps, they can do this at any time, whether or not a teacher is near. Soothing music (through headphones in class) may enhance the relaxed state. Students with learning difficulties can be taught this exercise using an audio recording or photographs of the steps.

Role playing. Role playing is a technique that helps students "try out" new behavior, language, and experiences with a teacher's support. For instance, if a student with emotional disabilities is being aggressive on the playground, the teacher may identify the situations that seem to trigger the behavior and then create scenarios of possible responses. If it is hard for the child to share, role playing might involve learning how to ask for a turn, and how to play cooperatively (e.g., helping turn a jump rope). Teachers can create or write the mini-dramas or let the learners set the scenes.

Visualization. Visualization is the controlled, directed, and purposeful art of envisioning a situation. It can be useful to any student in the inclusive classroom. "Seeing" oneself achieving a goal or behaving in a certain way has a way of making the brain believe that attaining that goal or behaving that way is possible. Students might visualize dealing with a bully, calming down during an altercation, or even managing anxiety before a test.

Suggest that students add details (the exact words they will speak and the outfit they will be wearing) and embellishments (background music, for example). The image needs to be a vibrant one that they can "view" over and over again and call up when needed.

7. ADAPT THE ENVIRONMENT

Some schools have a look and feel that inspires students to do their best. For instance, one elementary school we visited had appealing seating options like rocking chairs, kid-created art on the walls, spaces for quiet work and small-group interaction, boxes of sensory toys for anyone feeling "fidgety," and neatly organized (and easy to access) materials. In a high school we visited, the sense of safety and calm was related more to the school culture than to the actual surroundings. There were few rules—the motto of the principal was "few rules but high expectations." Students did not need hall passes, they used the honor system. During free periods, learners were encouraged to work together in comfortable little nooks designed for that purpose. In both schools, leaders saw their carefully crafted environment as a strategy for improving student behavior and performance.

Clearly, an environment can bring out the best or worst in students. Therefore, when examining an individual student's struggles, it is imperative to examine the student's surroundings. Also, keep in mind that while some examples of environmental changes are large and schoolwide (like those we just described), effective changes can be very minor. For example, a teacher who had a student with very sensitive ear drums asked all of his fourth graders to cut holes in four tennis balls and stick the balls on the feet of their chairs. This drastically minimized the noise created by thirty students moving their chairs all day and greatly reduced the stress and "difficult behavior" of the young man sensitive to noise.

Questions that can help us evaluate environment include:

- How does the noise level in the classroom impact the student?
- How, if ever, is music used?
- What materials are in the environment? Are they adapted for the learner? Age appropriate? Varied?
- What types of visual cues (e.g., pictures, drawings, written reminders) are in the work space?

- Is the lighting appropriate? Is it too bright or too dim for some learners?
- What seating options does the student have?
- Are the surroundings motivating, interesting, and created in part by students?

8. OFFER CHOICE AND CONTROL

All of us need to feel we are agents in our own lives. Even in small matters (what we eat, how we organize our workspace), most of us like to make as many choices and have as much control as possible. Having choices not only gives students a sense of freedom, fun, and belonging but also can head off discipline problems (Glasser 1990). It may be hard to believe that teachers can create more harmonious classrooms simply by asking students for their input more often, but it's true. Conversely, schools and personnel who do not give students a sense of choice and control will likely experience more challenging classroom behaviors from their students.

Giving students more choice is fairly easy considering all the moments in a day when there are options for participation, engagement, and response. Students can choose which assessments to complete, which role to take in a cooperative group, which books to read or which problems to solve, and how they wish to receive personal assistance and support. Other examples of choices that can be offered in classrooms are:

- Work alone or with a peer.
- Read quietly or write in your journal.
- Take a seat anywhere in the room.
- Conduct your research in the library or stay in the room and work.
- Type on the computer, write in your notebook, or go to the chalkboard.
- Choose any topic you like for your research paper.
- Select one of the three ways to be assessed.

Teachers supporting students who are experiencing difficulties should investigate how much control these students have in their day. In some schools, students who have a reputation for challenging behavior often have to earn the right to engage in preferred activities. This often has the unintended result of creating distrusting and frustrated students and exasperated teachers. Weaving preferred activities into the school day instead of offering them as rewards for performance or achievement offers a student comfort, predictability, and inspiration. Other questions related to control in students' lives include:

- What activities, environments, and materials does the student prefer? Does he or she have enough access to these things?
- Who does the student like? Does the student have time and opportunity to be with those he or she values?
- Does the student have free access to basic needs like food, drink, and privacy?

9. CHANGE CURRICULUM AND INSTRUCTION

While most conversations about behavior are centered on learners and their responses, needs, and challenges, teams seeking lasting change must look at how and what the students learn and how they are being taught. Bluestein (2001) states that the following experiences can be stressful for learners, especially those who already have difficulties in school:

- Being subjected to unrealistic or rigidly applied rules
- Being subjected to teacher impatience
- Being punished for moving, squirming, or doodling
- Having little variety in day-to-day curriculum
- Having an unpredictable schedule
- Being the recipient of unpredictable teacher responses (11)

Students who experience these challenges in curriculum and instruction may respond with "negative behavior." While teachers may not be trying to make the day difficult for certain students, and may not even be aware that they do, it is certain that some behavior is "inspired" by curriculum and instruction.

One common problem we see in both elementary and secondary schools is a mismatch between the curriculum and the students' interests and abilities. When students are struggling, especially in one environment or subject area more than in others, teachers should consider whether the content needs to change. Students may be struggling if the tasks are not appropriately challenging, if they take too long, or if they are boring, repetitive, or isolating. For instance, Sean, a sixth grader with Down syndrome, often had powerful tantrums when he was pulled into a resource room for reading instruction. Sean disliked being taken out of his classroom, particularly when he saw all of his peers gathering to discuss favorite books. His team soon realized that they needed to let Sean stay in his classroom, adapt the sixth-grade curriculum for him, and give him the same type of materials other learners were using.

Another common difficulty with instruction arises when the student's learning style doesn't match the teacher's preferred method of delivering instruction. If a teacher relies a lot on lecture, for instance, and the student needs a lot of opportunity for movement, the learner's unmet needs can result in problems for both parties. Teachers can alleviate this by determining student learning styles at the beginning of the year and acting on this information. Many of these challenges can also be averted if teachers differentiate their instruction, offering a wide range of lesson formats, teaching strategies, instructional groupings, and assessments throughout the year.

10. CREATE A SUPPORT PLAN

When a student does need a plan to address behavior challenges, make the document positive, student-centered, and comprehensive. While we *do not* believe there is any one way to write a plan, we *do* believe three elements are critical:

- Plan around abilities, not deficits. We often use a "strengths and strategies" assessment (Kluth and Dimon-Borowski 2004): a list of the person's strengths, talents, and gifts; and a list of strategies that we know work for the person (so we don't change things that are already working).
- Work closely with the student and the family. When possible, write the plan *with* the individual, not *for* him or her (Pitonyak 2005).
- Create supports that make the student's life easier and more enjoyable instead of focusing only on changing behavior.

We helped to write such a plan for Gavin, a learner with autism who was attending an inclusive school for the first time. During his first week, Gavin ran around the school, screamed, and bolted into classrooms, grabbing things that did not belong to him. Teachers were distressed and labeled Gavin a "behavior challenge."

However, when the team sat together to reflect, they generated several hypotheses for what might be causing Gavin's behavior. They realized that change is usually hard for a person with autism. They also realized that Gavin did not know much about his new learning environment; since he did not speak, he needed to gather information by exploring the school. And they admitted they did not know much about autism and probably did not have all the materials and strategies they needed to help their new student.

The more the team discussed Gavin, the more they saw him as a confused, scared, and somewhat undersupported little boy rather than as a problem. The team then looked both at Gavin's strengths (energetic, loves to play) and at strategies that were already working (giving him choices). They worked with Gavin and his family to learn about his preferences and their experiences. They then generated a variety of ideas for supporting him: giving him a bean bag chair (for sensory integration); teaching him a way to communicate; creating opportunities for movement (e.g., additional time on the playground); and providing educational materials that he preferred (e.g., books featuring his favorite animals, panda bears). All of these elements combined led to more peace, comfort, and success for the teachers and, of course, for Gavin.

Common Questions

I know it isn't politically correct to say it, but sometimes students need to know you are serious about dealing with the behavior. What about good old-fashioned punishment in certain cases?

One of the objections we personally have to punishment is that it doesn't teach students what to do; it only teaches them what not to do. Spanking a child, for example, can be very effective in stopping a toddler from fighting with his sister, but it will not teach him anything about sharing toys or using words to communicate. Therefore, it is likely the behavior will occur again. In addition, ironically, spanking the child may deliver the subliminal message that it is sometimes okay to hit other people to solve a problem.

Punishment is also limited in that it is simplistic and doesn't prompt us to explore the origins of the problem. A student who is punished for getting out of his seat repeatedly may thereafter stay in his chair, but if he was getting out of his chair because he craved movement or had another sensory need, he may feel anxious, restless, and unable to concentrate on the rest of the day's lessons.

Despite these drawbacks, teachers often use punishment because of the urge to respond in some way. One of our former students often kicked and bit staff members, and as the days passed without much change, so did the frustration and anger of the individuals supporting him. Even teachers who did not work with him directly felt frustrated and approached us to

suggest proper ways to discipline him. Clearly, the sch
munity wanted this student to be punished—not neces.
his benefit, but in order to "do something." Since staff n.~mbers
were being hit and kicked, they may have, consciously or
unconsciously, wanted this student to be punished as a
response to their being hurt. While it *is* certainly frustrating and
upsetting to be injured, punishing students typically does not
work. Nor does it make teachers feel better in the long run,
inspire new learning, or build classrooms in which all students
can feel safe and comfortable.

When, if ever, should a student be removed from the classroom?

We certainly understand that there are instances when students
may need to leave the classroom, particularly when they are
hurting others or themselves. The teacher should then, as
calmly and sensitively as possible, direct the individual to a
new space or environment and explain how and when they will
be able to return. It is our sincere hope, however, that these
instances are very rare.

We emphasize, however, that students should not be
escorted out of the classroom every time they struggle or every
time a teacher struggles *with* them. Too often, students with
disabilities are asked to leave the classroom or are escorted out
of educational environments without their permission. Faber
and Mazlish (1996) ask us to put ourselves in the place of a
student who is isolated: "As an adult you can imagine how
resentful and humiliated you would feel if someone forced you
into isolation for something you said or did" (115).

One way to avoid having to remove students from the classroom is to think preventatively and provide a "relaxation" space
for anyone needing one. There is absolutely nothing wrong—
and everything right—with having a safe, comfortable place
where any student can go to relax, calm down, and have a few
minutes alone. All students should be given this option, and
when a situation escalates or seems about to, the teacher can
ask the student whether he or she wants to use the space.

When at all possible, it is best to support and address challenging situations in the environments in which they occur.
Removing students from places where they should feel they

belong is detrimental to the building of community and, often, to the processes of teaching and learning.

Further, students need to learn to negotiate behavior in the most natural ways possible. Students cannot learn social skills without opportunities to make friends; they cannot learn communication skills without interacting and working with classmates; and they cannot learn competencies related to behavior if they are not allowed to solve problems and work through difficulties with others in authentic environments.

Finally, removing students from the inclusive classroom frames the behavior as the student's problem rather than as something that is socially situated. If a student is removed from the classroom, the teachers and the students are unable to see how the classroom community, the environment, the behavior of others, and the curriculum and instruction might be influencing that student's actions, feelings, movements, and moods.

I have a student who is really challenging. I feel like we have tried everything! What can I do?

The first thing to do is review anything that *does* work. Even if there is only a short window in the day when the student successfully maintains control, study this period of time as an anthropologist studies another culture! Explore it from all viewpoints, ask questions, and assume nothing. What happens during this period (even if it is only ten minutes) that is different from other times in the day? Whatever seems to be effective or successful or supportive might then be replicated in other parts of the day.

Another strategy is to expand the team. Consult a nutritionist if the student seems too lethargic, or an adult with a similar struggle who might offer an insider view.

Here are some other possibilities:

- Back off: do nothing.
- See the behavior from a different perspective. (For example, how would an artist, an athlete, or a scientist view the behavior?)

- Confide in the student to see whether she or he can help solve the problem.
- Videotape the child's interactions for a day to see if anything becomes clearer from this "distance."

Whatever you do, don't give up! There are countless stories of persistent teachers who have experienced breakthroughs with students deemed "unreachable." Our own story in this vein is about James, a student who ran from teachers, screamed loudly, and constantly hit himself and others. James initially had attended a special education facility. His classmates there were primarily nonverbal, and he was unaccustomed to classroom interaction. He had seldom been given materials to handle on his own, so he was unaware of a teacher's expectations in that regard. Also he had remained all day in one room, so changing environments made him anxious. However, after his team members united in sharing their ideas and offering support (e.g., teaching him sign language and assigning a peer tutor), James experienced many successes, including acting in the school play and joining the track team. He became such a popular student that teachers asked to have him in their classrooms! James teaches us not to give up, to instead face challenges with creativity and a commitment to our inclusive values.

References

Recommended Books

Brendtro, L., M. Brokenleg, and S. Van Bokern. 2001. *Reclaiming Youth at Risk: Our Hope for the Future.* Bloomington, IN: National Educational Service. The authors, through a blend of Native American childrearing philosophies and Western psychology, help the reader create a "circle of courage" to reach struggling students.

Clark, R. 2003. *The Essential 55: An Award-winning Educator's Rules for Discovering the Successful Student in Every Child.* New York: Hyperion. A book featuring dozens of "rules" that both inspire learning and keep the classroom peaceful.

Donnellan, A., and M. Leary. 1995. *Movement Differences and Diversity in Autism/Mental Retardation.* Madison, WI: DRI Press. Donnellan and Leary offer a unique perspective on understanding the bodies, behavior, and abilities of people with autism and significant disabilities.

Gilhooley, J., and N. Scheuch. 2000. *Using Peer Mediation in Classrooms and Schools.* Thousand Oaks, CA: Corwin Press. This very practical text features tips and examples related not only to peer mediation but also to conflict management in general.

Johnson, L. 2005. *Teaching Outside the Box.* San Francisco: Jossey-Bass. In her latest book, this popular teacher illustrates how connecting, common sense, and creativity can inspire classroom success.

Jones, T., and R. Compton, eds. 2002. *Kids Working It Out: Stories and Strategies for Making Peace in Our Schools.* San Francisco: Jossey-Bass. These authors examine common challenges and ways they can be constructively managed by, with, and for young people.

Kessler, R. 2000. *The Soul of Education: Helping Students Find Connection, Compassion, and Character at School.* Alexandria, VA: ASCD.

Kessler offers a succinct, inclusive, and sensitive guide to implementing character education with a strong spiritual focus.

Kohn, A. 1996. *Beyond Discipline: From Compliance to Community.* Alexandria, VA: Association for Supervision and Curriculum Development (ASCD). This book is a must for any teacher uncomfortable with the notion of "classroom management." Kohn offers sound advice for encouraging student cooperation and collaborative problem solving.

Lehr, D., and F. Brown. 1996. *People with Disabilities Who Challenge the System.* Baltimore, MD: Paul H. Brookes. This text is an edited volume written for those needing answers for students with autism, cognitive disabilities, physical disabilities, and health concerns.

Lovett, H. 1995. *Learning to Listen.* Baltimore, MD: Paul H. Brookes. This is a must-read for those teaching students with significant disabilities. Lovett reminds us to always put relationships at the heart of our work.

Marshall, M. 2001. *Discipline Without Stress, Punishments, or Rewards: How Teachers and Parents Promote Responsibility and Learning.* Los Alamitos, CA: Piper Press. You will find great suggestions for home *and* school environments in this book. Marshall's focus on reflection and self-evaluation make this text unique and worthwhile.

McGee, J., and F. Menolascino. 1999. *Beyond Gentle Teaching: A Nonaversive Approach to Helping Those in Need.* New York: Springer. In these pages, teachers will find sensitive, responsive, and, of course, gentle ways of responding to difficulties. This unique text focuses on teaching, learning, supporting, and understanding.

Recommended Websites

Disability Is Natural: www.disabilityisnatural.com

Instead of focusing on the problems or the label of a person, this site recognizes and celebrates the abilities, strengths, talents, interests, and dreams of those who have been labeled.

Gentle Teaching: www.gentleteaching.nl

An invaluable resource on the web! This site offers information on supporting people with behavior struggles, but it also helps teachers and others understand why some students *have* difficulties. The resources offered on this site help the user consider the quality of life and the human needs of those they support.

Imagine: Finding New Stories for People Who Experience Disabilities (David Pitonyak's Website): www.dimagine.com/page6.html

Imagine is the name David Pitonyak gives to his consulting practice, which is dedicated to supporting people with disabilities, especially those who are seen as having problem behaviors. This website contains helpful links to resources and many free and valuable articles on supporting people who are having difficulties in school and in communities.

Inclusion Press: www.inclusion.com

This website was designed and is sponsored by the individuals who developed and introduced Person Centered Planning to education and to those working in disability-related fields. This site contains products and information that will help teams conduct Person Centered Planning and create appropriate and hopeful supports for people with a wide range of needs.

Person Centered Planning Education Site: www.ilr.cornell.edu/ped/tsal/Enable

This website, like Inclusion Press, is focused on Person Centered Planning which enables people with disabilities to make choices and to be agents in their own lives. The site offers an overview of the planning process and a self-study course on this topic, readings, and helpful links.

Responsive Classrooms: www.responsiveclassroom.org/index.html

On this website, you will learn an approach to teaching and learning focused on student investment, responsibility, and learning. The best part of this resource-rich site is the newsletter where you will find information on respectful and friendly student behavior, increasing time on task, and tackling classroom challenges.

Ron Clark's Home Page: www.ronclark.info

Ron Clark, a Disney American Teacher Award winner, has assembled a comprehensive website complete with teacher resources and a very helpful message board. This site will be especially useful for those in urban schools dealing with issues such as overcrowding and budget problems.

Works Cited

Bluestein, J. 2001. *Creating Emotionally Safe Schools*. Deerfield Beach, FL: Health Communications, Inc.

Cautela, J., and J. Groden. 1978. *Relaxation: A Comprehensive Manual for Adults, Children, and Children with Special Needs*. New York: Research Press.

Faber, A., and E. Mazlish. 1996. *How to Talk So Kids Can Learn*. New York: Scribner.

Gallagher, P. A. 1997. "Promoting Dignity: Taking the Destructive D's Out of Behavior Disorders." *Focus on Exceptional Children* 29: 1–19.

Glasser, W. 1990. *The Quality School*. New York: Harper & Row.

Howlin, P. 1998. *Children With Autism and Asperger Syndrome: A Guide for Practitioners and Careers*. New York: John Wiley & Sons.

Johnson, L. 1998. *Two Parts Textbook, One Part Love*. New York: Hyperion.

Kluth, P., and M. Dimon-Borowski. 2004. *Strengths and Strategies*. Retrieved from www.paulakluth.com on October 30, 2006.

Lovett, H. 1996. *Learning to Listen*. Baltimore, MD: Paul H. Brookes.

Pitonyak, D. 2005. *10 Things You Can Do to Support a Person With Difficult Behaviors*. Retrieved from: www.dimagine.com on October 30, 2006.

You're Welcome

Collaboration

& Teaming

in the

Inclusive

Classroom

Patrick Schwarz
& Paula Kluth

HEINEMANN
Portsmouth, NH

To our fathers, Jimmy and Joseph,
For giving us the belief that doing good things
for people matters most.

Heinemann
A division of Reed Elsevier Inc.
361 Hanover Street
Portsmouth, NH 03801–3912
www.heinemann.com

Offices and agents throughout the world

Library of Congress Cataloging-in-Publication Data
Schwarz, Patrick.
    You're welcome : 30 innovative ideas for the inclusive classroom / Patrick Schwarz
and Paula Kluth.
        p. cm.
    Includes bibliographical references.
    ISBN-13: 978-0-325-01204-9
    ISBN-10: 0-325-01204-0
    1. Individualized instruction—United States. 2. Inclusive education—United States.
3. Group work in education—United States. 4. Multicultural education—United
States. I. Kluth, Paula. II. Title.

LB1031.S39 2007
371.9'046—dc22   2007016386

Editor: Harvey Daniels
Production: Lynne Costa
Cover design: Joni Doherty Design
Cover illustration: © Kevin Tolman/Photodisc/GettyImages
Typesetter: Kim Arney
Manufacturing: Louise Richardson

Printed in the United States of America on acid-free paper
11   10   09   08   07   CG   1   2   3   4   5

Contents

Acknowledgments

We are grateful to the many people who supported us to complete this project. Above all, we are indebted to the students with *possibilities* who have challenged us, taught us, and welcomed us into their lives over the years. We have been educated by many wonderful young people including Paul, Jason, Franklin, Tim, Mark, Jamie, Libby, Susan, Joe, Bob, Adam, Matt, John, Aaron, Andrew, and Bob.

The work of colleagues has also inspired this project, especially that of our dear colleague and friend, Alice Udvari-Solner. She has been a teacher to us for many years and constantly pushes our thinking on both the "what" and the "how" of inclusive education. Her work, in particular, on curricular adaptations and universal design of instruction is the inspiration for our own work in differentiated instruction. We must also acknowledge Mayer Shevin for his extraordinary work in the area of behavior supports; he has helped us dream bigger and understand how to work on problems and not on people. Also, we thank Barb Schaffer-Jaffe and all our colleagues at Kruse School who taught us countless lessons about collaboration, consultation, planning, and achieving change.

We are overwhelmingly grateful to our loved ones for supporting us and for allowing us time and space to do the work we love. We apologize for the endless conversations about inclusive schooling during dinner parties, evenings on the town, and at the concerts in the park—we can't help ourselves and you never roll your eyes or change the subject! We appreciate your enthusiasm

for our work more than you know. Thank you Todd, James, Erma, Willa, Rama, and Eden. We also wish to thank Mary, Peggy, Victoria, Vicky, Tim, Sarah, Bob, Katie, and Haley. You all *get it!* Our close friends and colleagues have also been witness to and supportive of our soap box at any given time, therefore, we pay tribute to Sandy, Buck, Kassira, Raul, Tanita, Howard, Tracy, Kevin, Eileen, Aria, and Kaitlynn. We also need to send a great big "gracias amigo" to Paco of New Rebozo. This book would not be possible without the inspiration provided by your wonderful tamales, moles, and ice cream surprises. "Oh My God!"

Finally, we send our gratitude to all at Heinemann and a great big "we are not worthy" to Harvey "Smokey" Daniels who had the idea to put a product like this on the market, allowed us to write it together, and coached us along the way. Thank you Smokey! A huge and continued thank-you also goes to Leigh Peake who supports us in countless ways and Lynne Costa is always a dream to work with. We anticipate and "welcome" many wonderful collaborations in the future.

Collaboration and Teaming

One day we walked into a school library and saw Joanne, a paraeducator from our team, quietly reading a book with a six-year-old boy. We watched them for twenty minutes, completely stunned. We had never seen this student sit still for more than six minutes. No teacher, therapist, or administrator had been able to help him relax so completely. Later, we had only one question for Joanne: "How did you do that?" She sat us down and told us the story of how the two came to be sitting peacefully and sharing *Miss Spider's Tea Party* (Kirk 1994) on that afternoon. She explained how she sang some of the sillier parts of the book (an approach her own son loved); used a voice so soft it was scarcely audible (which surely helped his fragile sensory system); and let him sit in the teacher's chair (which was extra-cushy). But Joanne also simply connected with this child, which is perhaps the most important lesson of the story.

In our work in inclusive schools we experienced many wonderful moments like the one with Joanne. We learned a lot from working closely with talented and committed professionals, paraprofessionals, students, and families. Often, when one person on the team did not have an answer, another one (like Joanne) did. We saw how some members of the team taught new competencies to other members simply by sharing work space and planning time. And we saw how innovation and ingenuity grew out of "great minds" coming together to share ideas.

Clearly, collaboration is no longer just a trend in education. Given the tremendous diversity in today's classrooms, teachers find that it is difficult to deliver effective instruction in isolation. Powerful teaching for all requires cooperation, teaming, and shifts in roles and responsibilities for many school personnel.

Of course educators are not alone in their pursuit of collaborative models. Even the corporate world has moved toward models that are more team oriented. Why? Because big business realizes that teaming increases productivity and creativity; the quality of work is better when it is done by teams. Teaming isn't something we do because it is trendy or because we have not yet learned enough about inclusive education to make it on our own. We collaborate because it forces us to grow as educators and because it will ultimately result in better outcomes for students.

1. EXPLORE COLLABORATION MODELS

In the literature on inclusive schools, four primary teaming models are highlighted:

- *Multidisciplinary.* This model is characterized by people supporting students in separate environments. Teachers teach in their classrooms, therapists provide their services in their offices, and so on. There is no ongoing planning; team members meet only when they are required to (e.g., annual reviews).

- *Interdisciplinary.* In this model, professionals serve students separately for the most part but find some common time for collaboration. For example, high school special educators may meet monthly to discuss student progress.

- *Transdisciplinary.* In this model, special educators and special services providers act as consultants. Some of the time students previously spent in separate places is replaced by observation, consultation, and evaluation in the general education classroom. There is ongoing planning. The advantage of this model is that therapeutic techniques get regularly supported and practiced in the classroom. For example, a physical therapist can come into the general education first-grade classroom and show the students and the teacher how to help a child with a physical disability work on the floor instead of sitting all day in her wheelchair.

- *Collaborative consultation.* With this model (Idol et al. 2000) any member of any team can act as a consultant for any other. For example, an occupational therapist may consult with a second-grade teacher about handwriting supports (wider lined paper, pencil grips) that can be used in the classroom. At the same time, that general educator may give the occupational therapist ideas for how she might work with several second graders who are writing in their journals, including the student with a disability. In this model, all the adults in the building are considering ways in which they might learn from one another, expand their roles and responsibilities, and share their expertise. No one person is *the* expert; all stakeholders are both teachers and learners.

We promote a collaborative consultation model because we feel it is the most conducive to inclusive education. Teams that use this model successfully report that while it is challenging to learn and maintain, it is the best one they have experienced and the most effective for serving diverse students.

2. Understand Teaming Stages

There are a variety of models that illustrate how teams come together and function. A favorite involves a play on words: *forming, storming, norming,* and *performing* (Tuckman 1965).

The *forming* stage takes place when team members are new to one another; it is typically formal, guarded, and watchful. (It is not an unpleasant stage, however, because people often treat strangers better than they treat people they know well!) The forming stage usually doesn't last long; teams move on to other stages as they spend more time together and learn how individuals in the group interact and approach their work.

As people get to know one another better, individual differences, philosophical differences, and ways-of-doing-business differences become apparent. This is often when groups begin *storming.* This stage can be characterized by conflict and, sometimes, confusion. The good news is that storming is entirely normal, unless the team seems unable to move past it and becomes dysfunctional. In these cases, strategies such as team-building, active listening, and problem solving may be employed. Some teams bypass this stage by planning carefully for change (e.g., introducing problem-solving techniques early in the process) and supporting one another as challenges arise.

The next stage is *norming.* Norming means that your team has learned to acknowledge individual differences and find a way to make processes work. Sometimes a team may agree to disagree about something. Typically teams in a norming stage are learning how to make meetings meaningful, how best to use what each member brings to the group, and how to maximize the resources that are available. Norming is a steppingstone to the most sophisticated and healthy teaming stage: performing.

A team in the *performing* stage has clear meeting processes, understands the needs and intentions of its members, solves problems effectively, listens to and learns from one another, and has a shared vision. In this stage, the group feels that no problem is too big for them to handle. Team members often have a common language and are able to get through their agenda with speed and efficiency. Performing teams are also student-centered and, in inclusive schools, they achieve outcomes on behalf of all learners.

Performing teams are essential in effective inclusive education. While it may take time, energy, and reflection to arrive at this stage, participants usually find that the destination is worth the journey.

3. DECIDE ON A MISSION

While team members will undoubtedly come to the group with different levels of commitment to and understanding of inclusion, they should share some core values about learners, teaching, and the school community if they are to reach all students successfully. To communicate these values, schools might craft a philosophy, creed, or set of goals that can be shared with all stakeholders (Thousand and Villa 2000). Staff members at Kruse Education Center drafted a mission for this very purpose (see Figure 1); they put their beliefs on paper to keep team members focused as they made decisions and to communicate the school's values to community members (Schwarz and Bettenhausen 2000). These elementary school teachers articulated beliefs not only about learning ("students of diverse abilities and educational background need to learn from one another") but also about what good support and teaching look like ("we need to empower students to be in general education settings whenever possible").

- Students of diverse abilities and educational background need to learn from one another.
- Our purpose is to find the "best way" of making education work well for students with individual differences.
- We can meet the needs of all students with diverse needs by individualizing the curriculum for the range of student abilities.
- Modeling is essential in learning.
- Support means more than just supervision. It means preparing to make informed educational decisions for all students.
- We own all students. Boundaries are minimized in our model.
- Most school- and community-based objectives for students with disabilities in primary and intermediate grades can be met in settings that include same-age peers without disabilities.
- We need to empower students to be in general education settings whenever possible, based on their individual needs and the degree they can tolerate the expectations or adapted expectations in the classroom.
- The focus of related service support is to provide expertise that will successfully integrate and enhance the general education curriculum.
- Every student is an "individual." Individual goals and objectives come first.
- The focus of learning is to make students more independent and empower everyone to be an effective learner and citizen.

Source: Schwarz, Bettenhausen, and Kruse Education Center staff (1994).

Figure 1   Philosophy and Recommended Practice Statement from Kruse Education Center

4. FIND PROBLEM-SOLVING TOOLS

No team is without problems. This is not necessarily bad news. Problems are normal and perhaps even helpful, because they can move thinking forward and keep team members flexible and creative in their work. The struggle for many teams, then, is not that they have problems but that they operate without an articulated approach to *solving* problems. Therefore, when issues build, the group may fall apart. For this reason, we suggest that teams have a few techniques for tackling challenges. The SODA approach (Schwarz 2006), summarized in the table below, is one we often use for problems both large and small:

S	**SITUATION**	Let's clearly define our problem so we can do something about it.
O	**OPTIONS**	Let's generate a wide range of possible options or solutions.
D	**DECISION**	From our list of options, which is the first we would like to try? (Let's also keep our list of options, just in case our first choice does not work.)
A	**ASSESS**	How did it work? Do we need to meet again or create an evaluation tool?

Another technique we have used is to reject a linear approach and tackle the problem from unique entry points (Harris 2002). Typically, teams begin at the beginning or "front end" of a problem. They brainstorm using the same strategies they have always used, and they often come up with solutions that look like solutions they have generated for other problems in the past. When teams vary the entry point of a problem, however, they may get more inventive answers. Consider, for instance, starting at the end of a problem. Trying to get money for a new school? Draw it, plan a garden, and even dream about what color to paint the walls. Then work in reverse and plot how you will gain community support. Or assume you are trying to figure out how to include a ninth grader with significant disabilities in general education. Instead of planning from the ground up by looking at the IEP and course catalog and trying to make matches, try looking at the finish line, which in this case would be a ninth grader without a disability label who has a typical schedule. Map *his* day, look for discrepancies (areas that would be hard for the actual student), and identify potential supports or adaptations.

5. BUILD YOUR TEAM

Teams are built through activities that strengthen relationships and allow them to grow. The goal of teambuilding is not to inspire close friendships between all members, although it's nice when that happens; rather, the goal is to inspire productive relationships and collegiality. Teambuilding also allows members to discover and value talents and gifts others have, which goes a long way toward being able to use these strengths on the team or as resources in other ways. This work, though often viewed as unnecessary "fluff" that gets in the way of real work, is anything but. When it is promoted well, teambuilding is a critical and effective tool for moving a team forward. Indeed, teambuilding has the power to *transform* teams.

Teambuilding or community building can be either formal or informal. Formal teambuilding uses preplanned activities to bring people together. Many teams use formal activities *only* during the initial meeting as an "icebreaker" and forget that teambuilding needs to be revisited regularly. For example, one school often used the game "Two Truths and a Lie" in their gatherings. (Each participant states three "facts" about his or her life and asks colleagues to guess which two are true and which one is false.) Over time, these teachers learned about the former and current passions, experiences, embarrassing moments, and dreams of their co-workers (the oldest faculty member "lied" about being an AARP member but had been a tango instructor and had once toured with a circus!).

Informal teambuilding activities are less structured, and groups have more choices and options. For example, the teachers at one high school had an open invitation after school on Fridays to meet at a local restaurant for refreshments and good conversation. In another district, staff members with a passion for reading set up a monthly book club. While some of the titles they chose were related to education, others were novels the members wanted to discuss for fun. A meaningful team activity is for the members first to list as many ideas as they can for informal teambuilding (coffee club, group morning walk, and so on), choose the options with the best fit, and integrate them throughout the year.

6. WORK AS EQUALS

In inclusive classrooms, the adults shift and share roles and responsibilities in order to give the students a wider range of supports, expand their own skills, and further their own knowledge. For example, during a writing lesson, an occupational therapist showed all of the first graders how to sit in their chairs properly and use a comfortable grip on the pencil, while the general educator worked with individual students. A paraeducator stood at the door of a secondary science classroom and collected homework, while the classroom teacher helped a student with physical disabilities set up his lab station. In other words, general educators are no longer the only ones delivering lessons, special educators are not the only ones supporting individual students, and paraprofessionals and therapists are no longer available only to a very few. All the adults take on different responsibilities and learn from one another.

While some teachers will find these changes refreshing, others may experience some anxiety. In such cases, up-front planning and discussion helps. One principal of an inclusive school shares how she helped teachers prepare for co-teaching:

> [I asked them], "So, how do you feel about sharing a room, having somebody else's desk in that room, and their stuff and their mess? What are you going to do the first time there is a behavior problem in the classroom? Who is going to do the disciplining? Who is going to make the telephone call home? How are you going to decide that? During planning time, do you co-plan? How many weekdays a week are you going to co-plan? How many days are you going to go separately and plan? . . . The message [behind those questions] was that I was not going to allow [one person] to act as an educational assistant in this classroom and the other person as the teacher. (Udvari-Solner and Keyes 2000, 443)

As this effective leader points out, collaboration requires parity between participants; colleagues need to demonstrate their willingness to work together as equals. Cook and Friend

(1995) suggest that adults working together in schools send parity signals—visual, verbal, and instructional—that convey equality in order to communicate their cooperation to others (11). For example, two co-teachers might host an open house night together, introducing themselves as a teaching team and each giving a short presentation to families. Other parity signals include:

- sharing teaching and planning space
- putting both teachers' names on the classroom door
- referring to learners in the classroom as "our students" (vs. *your* students or *my* students).

7. Embrace Co-Teaching

Co-teaching typically involves two educators jointly planning, instructing, and evaluating heterogeneous groups of students in general education classrooms (Walter-Thomas et al. 1997). By intentionally varying their roles, the co-teachers more fully share responsibility for their classes. Recent studies have applauded special educator/general educator co-teaching teams in preschool through high school classrooms (Meyers et al. 1991; Walter-Thomas 1997). In Meyers, Glezheiser, and Yelich (1991), for instance, general education teachers reported that they preferred in-class support to pull-out support because the more collaborative approach seemed to inspire a greater focus on instructional approaches for students with unique learning needs and resulted in more frequent team meetings. In a related study, educators in co-taught classrooms described themselves as confident about meeting the needs of all students in the classroom (Pugach and Wesson 1995). In addition, Walter-Thomas (1997) evaluated twenty-three co-teaching teams and found that both special and general education teachers reported that their collaborations had resulted in professional growth and enhanced their motivation to teach. In this same study, students claimed they received more teacher time and attention in their co-taught classrooms.

Two quick and easy ways to differentiate instruction and collaborate for two teachers are the one teach/one assist model and the one teach/one observe model:

- *One teach/one assist.* In the one teach/one assist model, the educators typically share lesson delivery responsibility, one leading, the other supporting in some way (Cook and Friend 1995). The lead person usually takes charge of the content, while the assisting teacher adds examples, shares humor, or takes notes on the board. The assisting teacher can also move through the classroom providing individual assistance and facilitating small group activities.

- *One teach/one observe.* In the one teach/one observe model, one educator leads or facilitates the class while the other sits back and watches how students respond. An observer might study whole-class dynamics (e.g., how students solve problems in collaborative groups) or individual student behaviors (e.g., how a student reacts to classroom noises, different ways a student communicates). Teachers can use this observational data to improve their planning and teaching and to learn about students in meaningful ways.

8. USE A RANGE OF CO-TEACHING STRUCTURES

Teachers can also deliver instruction together in more complex ways, like duet teaching, parallel teaching, and station teaching:

- *Duet teaching.* In "duet" presentations (Greene and Isaacs 1999), two teachers typically alternate the primary role in the classroom, taking turns leading class discussions, answering student questions, and facilitating lectures and activities.

- *Parallel teaching.* In parallel teaching (Cook and Friend 1995) the class is divided into equal sections and each group is taught the same lesson or does the same activity. This structure lowers the student-teacher ratio and "is useful when students need opportunities to respond aloud, to engage in hands-on activities, or to interact with one another" (7). Parallel teaching can also be used when teachers want to introduce smaller groups to two different activities, concepts, or ideas; the two instructors teach different content to separate portions of the class, then switch groups and repeat the lesson. (For example, a special educator teaches one group of fifth graders about the Democratic Party, while a general educator teaches the other group about the Republican Party.) Rather than have the teachers repeat the lesson, the students in one group can teach the material to the students in the other group and vice versa.

- *Station teaching.* "In station teaching, teachers divide instructional content into two, three, or more segments and present the content at separate locations within the classroom" (Cook and Friend 1995, 6). For instance, teachers might create four stations: one for listening to recordings of African drum music; one for collaboratively composing a few lines of music; one for learning a new drumming skill; and one for researching African music on the web. Station teaching is especially effective in classrooms served by several adults at certain points in the day. (See the accompanying book *Differentiating Instruction in the Inclusive Classroom* for more information.)

9. ENCOURAGE STUDENT COLLABORATION

Student cooperation and leadership is critical to the work of inclusive schools. When learners help their teachers create supports, develop rules, and draft goals, it is more likely that these things will be accepted, used, and understood by everyone in the school community. Collaborative roles that students can assume include:

- *Participating on the IEP team.* All students with disabilities should attend the meetings held on their behalf and share information and ideas to the extent possible. Students without communication difficulties can give a short speech, present a handout of ideas, or answer questions asked by team members. A student who cannot communicate reliably could push the button that advances the slides/photos in a PowerPoint® presentation about his life or simply hand everyone a letter from his family. If it is overwhelming for a student to be in a room full of adults, he or she can submit a report to the IEP team for self-advocacy purposes.

- *Becoming a peer advocate.* Since it can also be intimidating for students to be the only young person at an IEP meeting, they can be encouraged to bring a classmate along for a portion of it. This student can offer a "consumer's view" of curriculum and instruction, answering team members' questions or reinforcing the wants and needs of his or her friend with a disability.

- *Becoming a student member of a committee.* Adults often have conversations and make decisions that could be strengthened by student input. For example, a faculty team responsible for designing a new playground might get input from the student council before they draft plans. For their part, students can learn many important processes, such as how to fill out a survey and collaborate with adults.

- *Becoming a peer tutor.* Anyone, including students with and without disabilities, can be a peer tutor. Cross-age tutoring is especially popular in inclusive schools. For example, Sara, a second grader, tutors kindergarten students in math, which is an area of struggle for her. This tutoring relationship has boosted her self-esteem in this curricular area. Students might also serve as specialty-area tutors. For example, social-butterfly Patrick, a student with cerebral palsy who uses sign language, has become the peer tutor for sign language in his school. He goes to classrooms and teaches signs and, in return, his peers communicate back to him both at school and in the community. (See the accompanying book *Differentiating Instruction in the Inclusive Classroom.*)

10. Celebrate!

As a team we sometimes get down to the business of planning, teaching, and evaluating to such a degree that we forget to look at our accomplishments as a team and *celebrate*! The most effective teams, however, find ways to be reflective, pat themselves on the back, and enjoy one another's company. Smart teams know that celebration is one of the best ways to achieve healthy "performing" as a collaborative team. Here are some examples of how teams have found their way to celebration:

- One team typically assigns roles in their meetings: facilitator, recorder, reporter, timekeeper, encourager, jargon buster. Wanting to make their meetings more enjoyable, members now have a new role that rotates every meeting—*lavish praise distributor!* This person ends each meeting with *big* compliments and inspirational stories related to the team's work.

- Once a year, one team goes out for dinner and gambling on a casino boat. On the invitation, the team identifies all the areas it is celebrating that year (e.g., our students' reading scores are up, we were recognized as a high-performing school).

- Another team has an end-of-year picnic to celebrate accomplishments. Members bring their families. They also participate in games and activities.

- One school has an event, "Team Accomplishment Summit," to celebrate accomplishments at the end of the year. Each team shares what it has accomplished, and the school sponsors entertaining teambuilding activities and a luncheon. The accomplishments are published in the local newspaper.

Traditions, rituals, and enjoying time together are as important in schools as they are in families. Regular celebration helps inspire positive attitudes and high morale. Since inclusive schooling isn't always something for which schools get recognized (unlike high test scores, sports victories, or academic achievements), it is critical that educators themselves take time to recognize how very powerful and important their daily work, decisions, and commitment are to the lives of the learners in their care.

Common Questions

In order to support students and collaborate effectively, I know my team needs to meet regularly, but I have so many meetings I need to attend already. How do I find the time?

Finding time to plan for differentiated instruction and curricular adaptations may seem difficult, but it doesn't need to be. Be inventive, and let team members communicate what works best for them.

Some schools create the time by designating a planning day twice a month; on this day, the related services staff and the special educator keep their schedules free and a substitute rotates from room to room, so each teacher can meet with support personnel for at least a class period. Another way to encourage planning is to provide compensation to teachers who meet either before or after school hours.

Structural changes can be made to existing schedules to create or repurpose time for the meetings. A middle school that has daily grade-level team planning has a special education representative on each grade-level planning team. One day per week the entire team focuses on planning for diverse learners. In another school, "special studies" days were created on which the art teacher, the music teacher, and a paraprofessional worked with an entire grade level (eighty-five students) for ninety minutes at a time. Students had the chance to engage in unique cross-curricular projects (one-act plays, mosaics, song-writing competitions), while down the hall all three classroom teachers had the chance to plan curriculum and customized supports for all learners in the grade level.

Teams have also solved the time-shortage problem by tapping into school and community resources. For example, teachers have more planning time if they are freed from extra duties like lunchroom supervision. In one school, the principal enlisted parent volunteers to work in the cafeteria and on the playground so teachers could be free to meet and plan lessons.

I know storming is a normal stage of team development, but my team has remained in that stage and it is unpleasant. What should I do?

A team that lingers too long in the storming stage becomes dysfunctional. Two ways to move out of this stage are outlined in this book: teambuilding (get the group together to share time and experiences and to connect with one another) and problem solving (look for structured ways to examine challenges). Within these structures, there are techniques that can be used to build understanding and improve relationships.

Active listening is one such technique. Active listening means being empathetic and creating a safe climate in which to share problems or issues (Gamble and Gamble 2001); it involves using supportive body language, paraphrasing, and mirroring (keeping your tone and movement in sync with what the other person is doing). It should be done without judgment, put-downs, or advice. (A secret about advice is that people who don't ask for it probably don't want it.) The goal with active listening is supporting and strengthening relationships.

Another technique to improve collaborative interaction is to "pretend everyone is enlightened," a practice borrowed from the Buddhist tradition. Focus on what others are trying to communicate, instead on your own needs and purposes. Imagine that the team members are acting as they do solely for your benefit, to provide the teachings and challenges you need in order to learn and grow. While this practice may not get every team member to move forward, it can encourage multiple viewpoints, inspire creativity, and even bring a bit of fun to a difficult situation.

I am generally turned off by teambuilding. I think it is too "touchy-feely." Is it really necessary to engage in all those cute little activities?

Activities like these are part of formal teambuilding. In the book, we also explore informal teambuilding as an ongoing endeavor to support team members in a healthy way. There is a place for both in team development. Some people prefer certain types of teambuilding activities more than others; that's typical. Some teachers may prefer getting to know one another by attending district sporting events as a group, while others want more face-to-face conversation and "bonding." Letting team members have a say in the types of teambuilding activities they engage in is a good idea. Consider rotating teambuilding responsibilities among the team members so that everyone will have their preferences honored at some point.

Remember, too, that teambuilding takes place whenever we spend time together in new ways as we go about our day. Teachers who co-teach, for example, find that the daily rituals of sharing the morning coffee break, solving problems with their students, and delivering instruction side by side often brings them closer together and helps them become more familiar with each other's needs and talents. Therefore, another strategy for building a team is to look for opportunities to work with your colleagues in creative ways. For instance, in one school, a social worker who was feeling disconnected from her colleagues asked for recess duty because she knew that all the other educators had this job from time to time and often socialized while they watched the students.

References

Recommended Books

Cramer, S. F. 2006. *The Special Educator's Guide to Collaboration.* Thousand Oaks, CA: Corwin Press. While the authors include relevant research in this guide, the real gems in this resource are the practical exercises.

DeBoer, A., and S. Fister. 1995. *Working Together: The Art of Consulting and Communicating.* Longmont, CO: Sopris West. We love this resource for work in inclusive schools because it offers ideas for those in any grade level and for any number of consultative roles.

Doyle, M. 1997. *The Paraprofessional's Guide to the Inclusive Classroom: Working as a Team.* Baltimore, MD: Paul H. Brookes. Looking for ideas for hiring, supporting, and educating paraprofessionals? This guide is useful for staff development *and* for day-to-day practice.

Feigelson, S. 1998. *Energize Your Meetings with Laughter.* Alexandria, VA: Association for Supervision and Curriculum Development (ASCD). The title says it all! We love all of the ideas in this small but inspired book.

Friend, M., and W. Burseck. 2005. *Including Students with Special Needs: A Practical Guide for Classroom Teachers,* 4th ed. Boston: Allyn and Bacon. In their most recent edition of this popular textbook, these authors provide even more coverage of collaboration, with continued emphasis on student and family relationships.

Graves, D. 2006. *A Sea of Faces: The Importance of Knowing Your Students.* Portsmouth, NH: Heinemann. We can't claim to be collaborative in our schools unless we are connecting with students as well as colleagues. The personal reflections here are as valuable as the helpful hints.

Kinney, J., and D. Fischer. 2001. *Co-teaching Students with Autism.* Verona, WI: IEP Resources. The title is deceiving. This workbook-type resource does focus on co-teaching but also on adaptations, teaching strategies, and curriculum ideas.

Littlejohn, S. W., and K. Domenici. 2001. *Engaging Communication in Conflict: Systemic Practice.* Thousand Oaks, CA: Sage. Authors Littlejohn and Domenici discuss numerous methods in conflict resolution, including transformative mediation, issue framing, study circles, and dialogue groups.

Ruiz, D. M. 1997. *The Four Agreements.* San Rafael, CA: Amber-Allen. Be impeccable with your word. Don't take anything personally. Don't make assumptions. Always do your best. These are the four agreements! What else does one need to learn about collaboration?

Snair, S. 2003. *Stop the Meeting I Want to Get Off! How to Eliminate Endless Meetings While Improving Your Team's Communication, Productivity, and Effectiveness.* New York: McGraw-Hill. Snair shares ideas for streamlining communication, making meetings more efficient, and working with all members of your organization.

Snell, M. E., and R. Janney. 2000. *Collaborative Teaming.* Baltimore, MD: Paul H. Brookes. A comprehensive resource written primarily for those in inclusive schools.

Tamm, J. W., and R. J. Luyet. 2004. *Radical Collaboration: Five Essential Skills to Overcome Defensiveness and Build Successful Relationships.* New York: HarperCollins. We highly recommend this book for those looking for a fresh approach to teaming. It is a fun read full of practical advice and "radical" but easy-to-implement techniques.

Villa, R., J. Thousand, and A. Nevin. 2004. *Guide to Co-Teaching: Practical Tips for Facilitating Student Learning.* Thousand Oaks, CA: Corwin. The authors clearly outline co-teaching models and provide vignettes for teachers at every level. Readers will find the guides for lesson planning extremely valuable.

Recommended Websites

Circle of Inclusion: www.circleofinclusion.org

This site is a favorite of educators, administrators, families, and all others trying to create and maintain energy around inclusive schooling. The "methods and practices" section is perhaps the most relevant to those interested in collaboration; this segment features descriptions of schools that have used collaborative consultation and co-teaching.

Collaboration by Eduscapes: eduscapes.com/sessions/butter/
collaborate.htm

> The Eduscapes website allows teachers and students to develop
> web pages in order to share collaborative ideas around the
> world. It offers ideas for projects and provides a variety of con-
> nection resources and links.

Co-Teaching Connection: www.marilynfriend.com

> Dr. Marilyn Friend's website focuses on collaboration and
> provides co-teaching resources. Innovative practices are
> highlighted.

The Family Village Inclusion Resources—Global Community of Disability:
www.familyvillage.wisc.edu/index.htmlx

> A website dedicated to collaborative and inclusive practices
> around the world. This site offers something for everyone on the
> collaborative team, from health information to education con-
> tent to ideas for families.

Michael Giangreco's Home Page: www.uvm.edu/~ mgiangre/
index.html

> Perhaps the best feature of this website are the many links to
> Giangreco's own full-text articles on collaboration and support-
> ing diverse learners. Many of these are seminal papers that have
> set the standard for how to work with paraprofessionals and
> support staff in inclusive schools.

National Resource Center for Paraprofessionals: www.nrcpara.org/
node

> This website is key for paraeducators; it contains a long list of
> relevant research articles, information on upcoming relevant
> conferences, a blog that allows paraprofessionals to chat with
> one another and share ideas, and news on current related regu-
> lations.

Power of 2: www.powerof2.org

> This website, sponsored by the Office of Special Education Pro-
> grams (OSEP), is specifically designed to help schools move
> their collaborative models forward. One of the highlights of this
> information-packed site is the collection of FAQs (Frequently
> Asked Questions).

Richard Villa's Home Page: ravillabayridge.com

> Dr. Richard Villa is an innovative author, presenter, and con-
> sultant who features many collaboration resources on his web-
> site, including books, films, and information on upcoming
> conferences.

Works Cited

Bendtro, L. K., M. Brokenleg, and S. Van Bockern. 2002. *Reclaiming Youth at Risk: Our Hope for the Future*. Bloomington, IN: National Educational Service.

Cook, L., and M. Friend. 1995. "Co-Teaching: Guidelines for Creating Effective Practices." *Focus on Exceptional Children* 28: 1–16.

Fister, S., and A. De Boer. 1995. *Working Together: Tools for Collaborative Teaching*. Longmont, CO: Sopris West.

Friend, M., and L. Cook. 2003. *Interactions: Collaboration Skills for School Professionals*, 4th ed. Boston: Allyn and Bacon.

Gamble, T. K., and M. Gamble. 2001. *Communication Works*, 7th ed. New York: McGraw-Hill.

Greene, M., and M. Isaacs. 1999. "The Responsibility of Modeling Collaboration in the University Education Classroom." *Action in Teacher Education* 20: 98–106.

Harris, R. 2002. *Creative Problem Solving: A Step-by-Step Approach*. Glendale, CA: Pyrczak.

Idol, L., A. Nevin, and P. Paolucco-Whitcomb. 2000. *Collaborative Consultation*, 3rd ed. Austin, TX: Pro-Ed.

Johnson, D. W., and F. P. Johnson. 2000. *Joining Together: Group Theory and Group Skills*, 6th ed. Boston: Allyn and Bacon.

Kirk, D. 1994. *Miss Spider's Tea Party*. New York: Scholastic.

Meyers, J., L. M. Gelzheiser, and G. Yelich. 1991. "Do Pull-in Programs Foster Teacher Collaboration?" *Remedial and Special Education* 12: 7–15.

Pugach, M. C., and L. J. Johnson. 2002. *Collaborative Practitioners, Collaborative Schools*, 2nd ed. Denver: Love.

Pugach, M. C., and C. Wesson. 1995. "Teachers' and Students' Views of Team Teaching of General Education and Learning-Disabled Students in Two Fifth-Grade Classes." *The Elementary School Journal* 95: 279–95.

Schwarz, P. 2006. *From Disability to Possibility: The Power of Inclusive Classrooms*. Portsmouth, NH: Heinemann.

Schwarz, P., and D. Bettenhausen. 2000. "You Can Teach an Old Dog New Tricks." In *Restructuring for Caring and Effective Education: Piecing the Puzzle Together*, 2nd ed., eds. R. A. Villa and J. S. Thousand, 469–83. Baltimore, MD: Paul H. Brookes.

Thousand, J. S., and R. A. Villa. 2000. "Collaborative Teaming: A Powerful Tool in School Restructuring." In *Restructuring for Caring and Effective Education: Piecing the Puzzle Together*, 2nd ed., eds. R. A. Villa and J. S. Thousand, 254–91. Baltimore, MD: Paul H. Brookes.

Tuckman, B. W. 1965. "Developmental Sequence in Small Groups." *Psychological Bulletin* 63: 384–99.

Udvari-Solner, A., and M. Keyes. 2000. "Chronicles of Administrative Leadership Toward Inclusive Reform." In *Restructuring for Caring and Effective Education: Piecing the Puzzle Together*, 2nd ed., eds. R. A. Villa and J. S. Thousand, 428–52. Baltimore, MD: Paul H. Brookes.

Walter-Thomas, C. S. 1997. "Co-teaching Experiences: The Benefits and Problems that Teachers and Principals Report Over Time." *Journal of Learning Disabilities* 30: 395–407.